Praise for Jacob Watson and
Essence: The Emoti

In *Essence*, Rev. Jacob Watson rev
spiritual side of life, and ga
fulfillment. This is a beautiful, gentle, and wise book – a
marvelous gift to a world that is in great need of its message. I
know it will make the world a better place.
Larry Dossey, MD, author of *Prayer is Good Medicine*

Jacob's writing soars with holiness.
Gus Jaccaci, MAT, MFA, social architect

Essence is powerful and poignant. Jacob's subject matter is
compelling: the link between our emotional and spiritual lives. I
appreciate his sweet and user-friendly tone. It's very appealing.
Gregg Levoy, author of *Callings: Finding and Following an
Authentic Life*

Masterful, with wonderful distillations of experiences. Powerful
writing, as in such phrases as "painted this communion".
Arthur Fink, photographer and writer

In *Essence* Jacob Watson synthesizes and brings into soulful unity
all of who we are, giving grounded and practical methods and
examples to realize our innate being. I love all the examples he
uses and also his own prayers – lovely! It is a work that will
speak to many, being relevant to all spiritual traditions, or no
tradition at all.
Megan Don, author of *Meditations with Teresa of Avila: A Journey
into the Sacred*

Jacob's new book, which I highly recommend, shows how we can
claim complete responsibility for our own spiritual development.

Guiding questions offer focus; insight into establishing a time and place for spiritual practice offers inspiration; and powerful personal stories offer confirmation that crisis is a catalyst for spiritual progress.

Robert Atkinson, author of *Mystic Journey: Getting to the Heart of Your Soul's Story*

Wonderful book! His stories are fascinating, amazing and instructive, and provide a lightness as well as a groundedness to the material he presents. He opens the book with falling into the water and getting caught with his pants down.

Robert Zucker, author of *The Journey Through Grief and Loss: Helping Yourself and Your Child When Grief Is Shared*

I have full confidence and trust in Jacob, who is one of my most beloved workshop leaders. If anyone can help, it is him.

Elisabeth Kübler-Ross, MD

A vital, valuable and important book; clear, simple and compelling. His message is unmistakable and moving: he describes 'catching fire' in both literal and physical ways. His feelings blaze with authenticity and passion, some painful, some humble with grace.

Rev. Cindy Castleman, Hospice Chaplain

Jacob gets meditation just right: something that was already there. Most people are 'lost in thought' while meditation is about being 'found in silence'. He does a good job describing meditation as marvelous preparation for the activities of the day: that silence will tag along with us, especially after repeated practice. And I very much respond to the idea about one's emotional life leading naturally to one's spiritual life.

Dana Sawyer, professor of religion and philosophy at the Maine College of Art, author of *Huston Smith: Wisdomkeeper*

Essence is a gentle, sensitive, well-organized approach to communication with the divine that includes important but sometimes ignored elements of human emotions and the embodied self as expressions of prayer.
Rev. Corinne Martin

Jacob has drawn upon a lifetime of study and practice of wisdom traditions to synthesize, integrate, and present spiritual truths in a clear and useful manner. A wise and compassionate guide to novice and experienced seekers alike. A master teacher, Jacob offers gentle, direct, and understandable guidance on the path. There is a place of confluence of wisdom teachings and traditions. Jacob stands and speaks from that place.
Ron Feintech, PhD, Psychotherapist

His writing flows as gently as his voice, such a help for the heart! It takes us into another sphere where the dear heart is seduced into melting into Soul.
Phyllida Anam-Áire, author of *Let Love Heal: A New Consciousness for a New Age*

Part memoir, part learned treatise, part practical manual, *Essence* captures the considerable wisdom that Jacob Watson has absorbed in his many years as a spiritual seeker, practitioner, teacher and mentor. It is deeply felt, gracefully expressed and pragmatically structured to enrich the hearts, minds and souls of readers. A worthy addition to every spiritual aspirant's library of treasured books.
Philip Goldberg, author of *American Veda: From Emerson and the Beatles to Yoga and Meditation: How Indian Spirituality Changed the West*

Essence:
The Emotional
Path to Spirit

Essence:
The Emotional
Path to Spirit

Jacob Watson

BOOKS

Winchester, UK
Washington, USA

First published by O-Books, 2015
O-Books is an imprint of John Hunt Publishing Ltd., Laurel House, Station Approach,
Alresford, Hants, SO24 9JH, UK
office1@jhpbooks.net
www.johnhuntpublishing.com

For distributor details and how to order please visit the 'Ordering' section on our website.

ISBN: 978 1 78279 978 8
Library of Congress Control Number: 2014957343

A CIP catalogue record for this book is available from the British Library.

Design: Lee Nash
Diagrams: Marcie Watson

Printed and bound by CPI Group (UK) Ltd, Croydon, CR0 4YY, UK

CONTENTS

To my wife Kristine and our four children, Sarah, Kreschell, Alexis and Nate, and to our granddaughter, Adi.
And to Zoey.

Preface

The knowing of essence is love's secret.

– Rumi

Essence gets to the heart of things right away, just like poets. The Persian poet Jelaluddin Rumi is America's best-selling poet, and the reason goes beyond the immense appeal of his ecstatic poetry of love and passion. Rumi was born in 1207 in what is now Afghanistan, and later lived in Iraq. He walked the streets of Baghdad. Surely as the Western powers, at great cost, have poured immense resources into this anguished region for nearly two decades, we can harvest fruits of a different kind than regional influence, opium and oil. Rumi's vast writings – in fact they were dictations – shine forth profound teachings of love, forgiveness, wisdom and mercy. His passionate words shower us with permission to be free of rational restraints and encourage us to plunge into exuberance and ecstasy. The insanity of tribal and national warfare, and the greed and false promise of drug-induced ecstasy will fade into the past when we take up Rumi's challenge to admit the Friend – the Divine Presence – knocking at our door, here and now. This book begins with Rumi because he infuses wisdom into such few words, and these words describe precisely my intention for writing this book.

The word essence gradually emerged as the title of this book because it kept appearing both in my mind and on the pages of what I was reading. Essence signifies purification, a distillation; it stands for the core of things, the bottom line, the meat – or tofu – of things, the primary. It is a word that needs no adjectives; it has enough substance on its own. Once I decided on *Essence* for the title, it appeared even more in my reading. I did not know when I started to write this book that it would turn into the story of me finding my own essence, but it has.

As accurate as the word essence is to describe my subject and intention for this book, as we move from the world of emotion to the realm of spirit, language becomes a challenge. Choosing words to describe the material world, even the world of emotion, is easy. Our five senses give us ample information. But the spiritual world is unseen, and difficult to describe in words. Our attempts to do so bring forth uncountable names and symbols for what we call the divine and manifestations of the spiritual realm. In fact reciting them is a spiritual practice itself. This is notably true in the Muslim tradition of meditating on the ninety-nine "most beautiful names for God", and in St. Thomas Aquinas describing a litany of names for God from the Christian scriptures. In this book, I use a few of the more common names to describe the Holy One and the Holy Many or God. I wish to be inclusive, and expansive. I use words such as Divine, Creator, Holy Spirit, Nature herself, and, eventually, Essence. My hope is that the reader will find a name that resonates with his or her understanding, and that will inspire spiritual companionship. Also, I use the words emotion and feeling interchangeably, as they are used in the culture.

Though it is common for authors to search the literature to find appropriate quotations to place at the beginning of every chapter, I have not followed that form here. While the ideas in this book are grounded in both psychological and spiritual tradition, making ample quotations available, I want my words to stand on their own. Further, I see it as the reader's job and privilege to create his or her own references; this seems more beneficial. I encourage the reader to follow his or her own path to books, articles and Internet resources. Indeed, may the reader be inspired to write their own. To facilitate this, I suggest the reader keep a journal, or mark up the margins here to make these words relevant and remembered. Lastly, each chapter begins with a meditation, to set a tone of reverent inquiry, and ends with a brief Spiritual Practice that uses the theme from that chapter.

Foreword

In the stream of life we often focus on the rocks and miss the water flowing all around them.

One sunny spring day I was driving to give a workshop on end of life care to the staff of a rural nursing home. I found it right away and had time to spare. I drove past the home and came to a quiet bridge where I stopped the car. I got out to enjoy the peaceful stream flowing under the bridge. I looked down at the water tumbling over the rocks, and was reminded of the saying quoted above. I remembered that I happened to have my camera with me. I climbed down the embankment with my camera in hand and stood in the shallow water at the edge of the stream. The scene was just as I had imagined when I wrote the above words. I took several photographs then stepped further into the stream to get a better shot. Suddenly my foot slipped and I fell into the water up to my knees. I scrambled back to the bank. My camera was wet, but the most immediate problem was that I was due back at the nursing home to teach a workshop in a few minutes and my pants were dripping wet and muddy. I climbed back up to my car, got in and turned on the heater. I took my pants off and held them up to the heater vents. Just when my pants seemed to be getting dry, I saw a big orange school bus drive up right behind me. The doors opened and some kids began to get out. I scrunched down in my car seat hoping they wouldn't see me without my pants. I could just imagine trying to explain myself to the school bus driver, or worse, a county sheriff. Luckily the kids walked across the road, and the bus drove off. I pulled on my pants, which were still damp, but wearable. Soon, I was at the nursing home to start the workshop. I'm sure I looked disheveled, but no one said anything. Later, I salvaged the film from the camera and used the image of the stream flowing around the rocks on my Web site. I realized I needed to fall into the river to get the message that the spiritual life is all around me. In fact, I am soaked in it.

Introduction

Meditation:

Precious, precious time;
Oasis for the thirsty soul.
Drink this deeply.

When I was twenty-two, I saved up some money from my first teaching job and bought an old 21′ wooden cruising sailboat in Connecticut. I named it Wandoo, a child's version of 'I want to', in honor of my passion to sail and my grandfather who had a boat named Wanderer. The name was also in celebration of finally owning my own boat, something I'd wanted to do ever since I began crewing sailboats for my cousins as a little boy. With my girlfriend along as crew, I sailed my new boat down the Connecticut River, and east to Buzzards Bay where I had grown up sailing. It was a rough trip: the cotton sails were stretched out of shape, and the engine was old and unreliable. But I was young and ecstatic to have my own boat, and to sail it home to the harbor and shore-side house where I grew up in the summer. For days we sailed along the coast and came in every night to a sheltered harbor. Then, feeling triumphant, my girlfriend and I finally anchored the boat off my parents' house. When we rowed ashore, I saw the 'big rock' on the beach. It had for years been a favorite place for a local blue heron to stand and fish in the shallow water. My cousins and I spent countless hours wading out to it at low tide when it was fully exposed. At high tide it was completely covered and we would swim out to it and climb up on the slippery top. Other childhood memories swirled around me as we walked up the dock. My parents welcomed us, sort of, and after supper we rowed back out to the boat at anchor. A few hours later after we had crawled down into the cramped berth and gone to bed, I heard someone approaching in a rowboat.

Then I heard my father calling to us. "I think you'd better come in for the night." Reluctantly, we rowed ashore and my mother invited us to sleep in separate bedrooms. I hardly slept. The next morning after breakfast when my girlfriend and I started down the lawn to re-board my sailboat, my mother started screaming at us. I'd never seen her like this. All her rage about us living together without being married came pouring out, mostly at my girlfriend. My mother told her she couldn't walk across the family property. I was stunned into silence. I was hurt, embarrassed and ashamed. I ignored my mother, and pointed to a neighbor's dock. I told my girlfriend to walk over there, and told her I'd pick her up with the boat. I had no words to say to my mother; I just walked away. We sailed out of the harbor, eventually to Maine. About a year later, still feeling protective of our relationship, my girlfriend and I were married by a Justice of the Peace. I did not go home again for almost three years. During that time I came to understand that my path led away from the sheltered harbor where I grew up. Even though I did not yet have the language to describe what I felt, I could take the actions necessary to lead my own life, to steer my own ship.

This book is the story of how I have been healing from this and other wounds, and how I have come to understand and celebrate the ways in which my natural emotional life led to my natural spiritual life. It is a chronicle of my personal journey from WASP, White-Anglo-Saxon Protestant, to Blue Heron – yes, that heron standing on the 'big rock' of my childhood. A wasp is small, brittle, a nest-dweller, buzzing erratically in flight, and has a nasty stinger. A blue heron is large, tall, a shore-wanderer, a creature who is at home where boundaries meet. It is thin and ungainly, but at the same time graceful, especially in flight. It is mostly quiet, but occasionally erupts with a ragged squawk. Familiar with these qualities, I have long identified with Great Blue Herons. They show up in my life in auspicious moments, arcing over the road in front of me, or tracing a silent low swoop through a marshy shore. Over the years, Great Blue Herons serve as accurate symbols of my journey from a shy, sheltered, uptight, privileged youth into a grateful, if not always graceful, independent adult. My feet are still sometimes stuck in the mud, yet I seek flight and transcendence. In an early awkward attempt to fly solo, I signed up for a Gestalt therapy personal growth weekend. The opening exercise required each of us to go around the group and describe briefly to each of the ten participants a childhood wound. I did so, but I had a difficult time looking at anyone directly. When I finished, I was shocked to see that they all still sat there, looking at me, and with their calm gazes offered me acceptance and love.

I have been able to work to heal my wounds – a lifelong process – with life experience, therapy, workshops and trainings, and from the many insights of workshop leaders, teachers, authors, grieving clients, my students and friends. I remember years ago my embarrassment, sitting at lunch with a fellow college student, when I shared that I did not have any friends. His face crumpled and he said, "Well, I thought I was your friend." My reassurance did little to change his hurt, and I knew I had a lot to learn about friendship. Yes, I wanted friends to do things with, but increasingly I sought friends and teachers who appreciated and would explore the mysteries of life, the 'being' side of life, the spiritual dimension of things. This, then, has become my life's work: to work with emotional and spiritual growth, my own and others', counseling, creating schools, workshops and trainings. This is the realm of essence, to live in the present, to acknowledge and then express natural emotions and therefore one's natural spirit. The results are authenticity, personal growth and development, and contributions to the healing of a suffering world.

When I began to write this book I asked myself: Why am I writing it? Why would anyone pick this book up and read it? Can a book change a life, many lives? And why do I want to change a life? Don't I think that a person's life is good enough for them? And who am I to want to change another person's life, and what business is it of mine, anyway? Why isn't their life good enough, right now? The answers came slowly, as if out of the Maine fog (see the Fog visualization in the Afterword). But they came powerfully, and with grace and emerging clarity: I want to share my experiences and what I have learned, to make a difference, maybe to ease someone's suffering. Even if my words comfort only one person, that makes it worth it. Faith and trust are called for.

Spiritual teachers tell us that in our brief existence here on earth all we have is now, this precious moment. Here and now, you have the courage to pick up this book. Be aware of your fingers holding this book, your eyes reading each word, perhaps a taste in your mouth, a smell in the air. This is it, life experienced as consciously as possible in this moment. Our consciousness and what flows from it are so abundant that you might even be thinking a separate thought while you are reading. As Deepak Chopra reminds us, our body can at the same time track multiple rhythms, heal from a disease, grow a baby, mend from a bruise, grow new cells, digest food, plan a lunch date, feel sad over a recent loss. This is the principle of simultaneity. Here you are right now, unconscious and conscious. But who is it, really, that is holding this book, noting the information being delivered by your five senses and your intuition? We will move through these chapters with the goal of answering that question. I seek to facilitate your healing and conscious evolution into the deeper and deeper realization of your consciousness, your natural emotions and how they awaken your spiritual state of being, your essence.

It is 3am and suddenly I am wide-awake, and for a moment I have brought my essential self back from dreamland. My mind is not yet cluttered by everyday life. On the very last page of Michael Ventura's book *Shadow Dancing in the USA* he writes, "At 3am sometimes in the darkened house across the street, one light goes on. Someone else is tired of being asleep. We are each other's answers. We always have been and always will be." I've used those words over and over in my workshops. Many is the time, especially because my usual side of the bed is nearest the window, that I have been awakened by the moon, full or close to full, shining its warm light down through the window onto my face, gently touching my skin with its sweet caress. The sudden otherworldly touch of creation – of enlightenment – wakes me up, infusing me with a familiar memory of being an integral part of all this, in here, the warm bed, out there, the cool night. This is a precious moment-to-moment experience of consciousness. I *am* tired of being asleep – in the many variations of asleep.

Often I get up and write, or mediate, or pray. This is how I connect: "We are each other's answers," and how I reinforce my sense of belonging to the Divine. Breathing softly in and out, I am reminded that I need not do anything but accept and receive this special graceful illumination and encouragement. In this silent moment that encompasses eternity I know from my depths that this glowing moon and I myself are one and the same creation of the Universe.

May you harvest the teachings and ideas in this book for your own growth, understanding, healing and enlightenment. May you use this book as your personal workshop manual, to harvest in your own way, in your own time, and for your own purpose. My earnest hope and my passionate wish is that you begin – and continue – to intuit, recognize and value above all else who you really are, your unique authentic natural emotions, your spiritual presence and the special gift of your unique essence. May you, a spiritual being in human form for now, give this gift of essence first to yourself, and then to all Creation. May you wake up to the fact of your conscious existence, the fact that you are consciousness, that you are spirit. May you join me, as I join you. Let us be companions on this journey to essence.

Spiritual Practice: "Enough"

Find a safe and quiet space to inhabit. Introduce yourself to who you are at this time and in this place. Speak your name out loud. Then say, "Who I am and what I'm doing – or not doing – is enough." If you'd like a word to focus on, a mantra, that word can be 'enough'. "I am enough." This practice is to do nothing, not even meditate, not even sit in a particular way nor breathe in a particular fashion. This practice is not to change a thing, only to bring a quiet, soft, relaxed acceptance to exactly how you are at this moment in time, reading these words, wherever you are in your life right now. Say it again, "I am enough." That's all, no change, simply being enough.

Part I

Doing Our Work

Chapter 1

The Four Quadrants: A Healthy Balance

Meditation:
I sit with my body.
I sit with my feelings.
I sit with my mind.
I sit with my spirit.
Such fine companions!

I first saw the diagram describing the Four Quadrants when Elisabeth Kübler-Ross drew it up on the wide green chalkboard in the main conference room at the Notre Dame Spiritual Center in Alfred, Maine. I was attending her "Life, Death and Transition" workshop, eager to improve my skills as a grief counselor. Set on a rural road, the Center used to be a Shaker community and now was a retirement residence for Catholic priests who had served as schoolteachers around the world. The brothers maintain the buildings and grounds and grow much of the food they serve to retreat guests. A gentle spiritual aura surrounds the rustic buildings, fields and apple orchards. Though I was nervous about the workshop, I felt at home walking in to the comfortable spaces. Little did I know I'd be returning there for 30 years!

To see the diagram of the Four Quadrants on the chalkboard gave me a needed visual picture of ideas that helped me understand my life. It also was useful to use in my counseling practice as my clients worked through their grief and other natural emotions. In that first day of her Life, Death and Transition workshop, Elisabeth, with her Swiss accent, presented the Four Quadrants as a model of health: the Physical (Body), the Emotional (Heart), the Intellectual (Mind) and the Spiritual

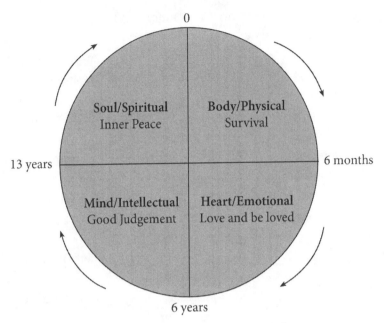

The Four Quadrants Model:
Health = Balance

(Soul). She explained that this is similar to the Four Elements of Earth, Air, Fire and Water, and the Four Directions used by various Native traditions. Elisabeth made it clear that this model is not to be used as a rigid formula, but rather as a gentle diagnostic tool to clarify the relative balance of our different parts, and thus identify how we might regain the health of equilibrium. She said we consider these parts in order to better understand and support the whole person. Holistic health demands and seeks balance. To create balance creates health.

Health

According to this idea, in response to what life gives us our Four Quadrants get out of balance – voluntarily or involuntarily. We can voluntarily choose to concentrate on one quadrant, for example the physical. To care for our bodies, we might exercise more, get more sleep, and eat a more healthy diet. We might decide to concentrate energy on the emotional quadrant to care for our heart, to heal an emotional wound from years ago, or from yesterday. We might feel and express our outrage and anger at being somehow mistreated. To care for our mind, we can choose to activate the intellectual quadrant. We might research a topic that intrigues us, or learn to solve a problem, or enroll in an educational class or school program. To care for our soul, we might choose to expand our spiritual quadrant. We could seek spiritual experiences, read scripture or mystical teachings, go on pilgrimage, or engage in practices such as meditation, prayer, or worship in a temple, church or mosque.

Then again, life happens, events take place whether we like it or not: we lose our job, our partner ends our relationship, or we get sick. Or perhaps we experience an unexpected moment of ecstasy. Involuntarily we lose our balance. One quadrant demands attention. Then we try to adjust in order to handle the immediate mystery, stress or crisis. That's OK short term; it takes time to return to our balanced state. For a while we find ourselves off center, confused, out of balance. We can use this model of the Four Quadrants to explore these four major parts of our being, and develop a deeper and more practical understanding of them, their function and relation to the whole, and move towards a balanced and healthy self. Now we will consider their developmental flow. We will look at how each quadrant originates, and how, with self-forgiveness, we can return to a more organic and balanced state to be whole. Which quadrant is calling for more attention and energy? How can we give it what it is calling for? How will we create more balance and wholeness?

Body – The Physical Quadrant

When we are conceived, a sperm meets an egg, and we begin our physical journey here on this planet at this time and in this place: the miracle of conception and birth. Suddenly we are physical, the first of the Four Quadrants. Spirit has become matter. We have a body. Unconsciousness has become Consciousness. We have incarnated, embodied, become flesh. In uteri, and during the first few months of life after birth, the developmental emphasis is on the physical quadrant. The developing function centers on the five senses, sensation itself, and the purpose is physical growth and security. Because we are human we have fleshly needs. Our body needs to be protected from danger. The basic need is survival. The helpless newborn infant must be sheltered, clothed, fed, changed and nurtured. If this happens, then we thrive, grow and mature. We develop security about having a body, and about being here on the planet in physical form. Ideally we learn that our bodies are sacred: a temple to be respected and cared for. We learn to listen to our bodies, to hear and feel what they require for health and well-being. But if we are not sheltered, not cared for or not respected physically, then we experience wounds, painful wounds that our bodies remember. Fears and phobias arise from physical harm. As infants, some of us were hurt, abused, and damaged physically. Some of us were abused sexually, inflicting physical, emotional and spiritual wounds. Perhaps we found ourselves in the care of adults who hurt us and it took us years to recover. Though we cannot erase our history that includes physical wounding, some of the effects of physical wounds can heal. Most physical wounds leave an emotional scar. It is important to learn that with the support and expertise of friends, therapists, healers, workshops, books – our own hard work – we can revisit old wounds later in our lives and provide ourselves with healing and forgiveness. Here lies the relief of inner security, to know and trust that we – our physical bodies – have a rightful place in the world.

Heart – The Emotional Quadrant
Around six months of age, the emphasis turns to the development of the emotional quadrant. The growing function is

facility with emotions and feelings, and we begin to gain ease, experience and skill to express our emotions. The purpose is self-care and the development of relationships, including with ourselves. The need here is to belong, to love and be loved, both. Naturally, we cry when we're sad, we yell and scream when we're angry, we get anxious when we are afraid; we smile and giggle when we're happy. If our emotional expressions are noticed and affirmed – responded to – we develop trust and confidence that it's OK to express our feelings, and that our feelings matter. When we're hungry and cry for food, if our caregiver hears us and responds – by bringing our mother's breast, or a bottle – then over time we develop confidence and a sense of security in the validity of our emotional self. We learn that to express our feelings has consequences, and that other people care about us enough to respond. Thus we come to understand that we are part of the human community of people who care about each other, who respond to each other's needs. To learn that relationships are a two-way street is the start of learning how to be in relationship with each other; relationships must have response-abilities built in if they are to be successful. When we get caught in *reaction*, we pay more attention to the other person than to ourselves; if we *respond* we retain our personal choice to accept our own feelings.

Of course, we can be wounded in the emotional quadrant too. Incompleteness here brings feelings of rejection, abandonment and betrayal. A parent can be judgmental, dismissive, scornful, insensitive to our natural emotions, and thus create a wound. A father or mother, or other caregiver, can be so consumed by their own needs that they have no room to attend to a needy infant. They might tell the child to shut up, to stop crying. They might demand quiet or expect certain behavior from us. As we grow into adults, a major task of claiming our personhood is to regain the ability to acknowledge and to feel and express our natural emotions. As this skill develops we grow into self-acceptance and self-love. Working with the ideas, meditations and spiritual practices in this book will help develop more skill and confidence to express feelings, thus creating honest and healthy relationships with ourselves and with others in the world. We can then feel the relief and exuberance of feeling our true feelings and being our authentic and essential selves.

Mind – The Intellectual Quadrant

Around six years of age, as we learn to figure out how to get our needs met in the larger world, the emphasis turns to our intellectual development. The growing function is thinking and reason, and the purpose is intellectual development. We need to know, to use reason to figure out how the world works. An organic feedback loop develops to inform us whether or not what we do is effective to get our needs met. If our action is not successful, if it does not produce the outcome we seek, we modify it to achieve better results. Our intellect helps us do this, helps us remember what actions are successful, and what actions are not successful. We learn how to investigate; we use our mind to do research to find the information we need. We ask other people, learn in school, read books, and use the Internet. In this quadrant, too, wounds can occur, as when we are criticized as intellectually lacking or incompetent. Incomplete development here means feeling stupid, dumb, inadequate, and incompetent and even feeling crazy. We may start school, or visit a friend down the street or across town. What if our dad forgot to pack our lunch? What if a playmate teases us? After we feel our feelings we might have to do something, take some action. Our mind, our intellect, can help us decide what to do and how to do it. When we forget our homework assignment or can't come up with a correct answer, perhaps a teacher ridicules us in front of the class. Our classmates might call us stupid. Humiliation creates a profound wound. Again, this might be our history, which we cannot change. But over time we can recover, heal and regain a sense of intellectual confidence and competence. This allows us to move forward in life exercising good judgment. With practice, we can develop our intellectual capacity to help us get our needs met in the world.

Soul – The Spiritual Quadrant

During the teen years, the emphasis shifts to the spiritual quadrant. Here the function is intuition and the purpose is spiritual growth. We begin to notice that family members and friends may express their spirituality by attending temples or churches. Often popular culture, in movies, TV shows, the Internet and music, brings us references to spiritual ideas. The need is to develop curiosity about life's major questions, and to seek connections with our creator. Around puberty, at 12 or 13 years old, and onward, we begin to ask questions that are spiritual in nature such as: Who is in charge of things? Why do bad things happen to people? Why do people have to suffer? What control, if any, do I have of my life? Am I really as alone as I sometimes feel? Is there a God or higher being or Spirit, and if so, do they care about me? When we know that these are normal and healthy questions to ask, then we develop a sense of confidence about having a spiritual life. We grow into the realization that we are a spiritual being.

The Indian Raid

When I was around ten years old, my family moved to a new state to live. Once we got settled, my mother took me along with her when she went to look for a new church. I wondered if God was to be found in all these different churches. Did God have other names? We ended up attending a Quaker Meeting, where our Sunday school class sat with the adults for the first part of their silent Worship. We met in an old stone building built in the 1700s. There I heard the story that in colonial times the Quakers met one First Day (Sunday) and an Indian war party burst screaming through the door. The Indians encountered the room full of Quakers sitting in silence. None of the Quakers moved. They remained sitting on their wooden benches that faced each other; they did not get up or speak. The raiders looked around, then left quietly, leaving the worshippers in their silence. I was deeply impressed by this story, which became part of my family's precious few conversations about spiritual life. Why did the Indians leave? Weren't the Quakers scared? I realized even then the lesson that something was more powerful than fear. I was impressed by the image of the room full of Quakers, a room I came to every Sunday morning, sitting there quietly even while threatened with harm. This was the first time I had been a member of a group who consciously not only refrained from speaking, but also who valued the resultant silence. The lesson went deep into my young soul: silence has power.

How Illness affects The Four Quadrants

Now let's look at what happens to the four quadrants when we have an illness. Illness means the physical quadrant is compromised, or in pain. Sometimes it is literally diminished by surgery, as when a cancerous tumor is removed. Our physical abilities and capacities may become limited; we may not be able to function in our usual ways, or to lead our normal lives. We discover new restrictions, and often have to redesign our daily life around them. Our perception of who we are can change, too: our relationships to our family, friends, work colleagues, and to the world at large. Sometimes we get so identified with our illness that we use it to define ourselves. Meeting a person for the first time we may say, for example, "I have Parkinson's", or "I am a cancer patient."

Sometimes the illness, like cancer, is life threatening, and the physical quadrant changes more dramatically. With a diagnosis of a terminal illness, suddenly the ground shifts under our feet. All the quadrants become unstable as we swing wildly from one

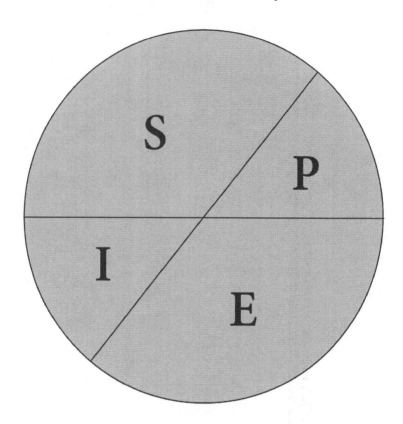

With Illness

quadrant to the other, from extreme emotions to new spiritual questions, even while we focus energy, time and resources on the physical quadrant. We work and hope for improvement and healing. If we find ourselves living in this kind of chaos, it can be helpful to use the diagram of the Four Quadrants in order to create better balance for ourselves. When the physical quadrant calls for attention, it is important to give it energy. Illness stimulates the other three quadrants, too. How can the other quadrants serve as supports to address and care for the physical illness?

If the illness is mental, then the intellectual quadrant may be compromised and less capable of researching and processing information, of handling everyday tasks and challenges. Our ability to recall past events is reduced; we struggle to plan adequately for the future. A common example is early dementia or Alzheimer's. We may feel frustrated and angry that we cannot remember what happened yesterday, recall the names of our own family members, or remember how to feed or toilet ourselves. We may no longer be able to cook, or to drive a vehicle. Indeed, we may require a round-the-clock caregiver, or need the support of an assisted living facility or nursing home to provide 24-hour care.

When this happens, we have a great deal of feelings about having these illnesses, new limitations and challenges, whether they are physical or mental. The Four Quadrants adjust accordingly. As the physical quadrant shrinks, the emotional quadrant grows. We feel a lot about what is happening to us! In response to a threat, or a reduction of the physical quadrant, it is helpful to identify and express our Natural Emotions. In addition, the spiritual quadrant grows because our illness generates spiritual questions such as, "What is the meaning of my life now that I have cancer?" "Why did God allow this to happen to me?" "Who am I now that I can't remember my past?" Often we want to engage in these spiritual discussions and seek spiritual counsel. Thus, we see the healing quality of flexibility in the Four Quadrant model. When one quadrant shrinks, others grow to show us what is needed, and point out where we need to focus our attention in order to recover the health of balance. This model reminds us that no matter how the quadrants shift in response to what comes our way, or what changes about our lives, we are always a whole person. All of life's experiences, both inner and outer, past and present – are contained and held in the circle. Now let's look at how Western culture views the four quadrants. The diagram for our culture looks like this:

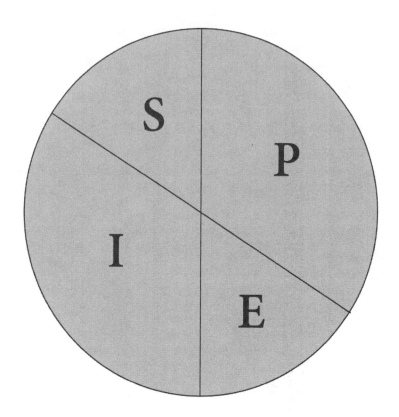

Our Culture

Our Culture's Version of The Four Quadrants

Our culture, as manifested in the messages we receive from our parents, schools and media, supports the physical and intellectual quadrants at the expense of the emotional and spiritual quadrants. This results in a person, and a culture, that is way out of balance. Indeed, we are so out of balance that our culture has lost its soul. If we become so concerned with our physical and our intellectual selves, then we have little time and energy to inhabit our emotional and our spiritual selves. We pay our sports heroes, those who perform well physically, multimillions of dollars a year to swing a baseball bat, throw a football, or shoot a basketball. We reward our movie and television actors, who embody our culture's standards of beauty and celebrity, with millions of dollars per film or TV series. Also, our culture prizes the intellectual quadrant: we reward people who are smart; we promote education and compensate people based on how many letters (degrees) they have after their name. However, please remember that the culture is not all 'out there'. Yes, we are influenced by cultural norms, but we help create the culture. We can be more conscious and responsible as creators. Especially in concert with others (see Chapter 13) we can change the culture in which we live.

This excess concentration on the physical and intellectual quadrants, when considered in the context of a whole and balanced person, can diminish energy, growth and expression in the emotional and spiritual quadrants. We can become obsessed with our bodies, punishing them to meet what we think are the culture's norms. Or we live in our heads, believing we can use our intellect to figure out all of life's problems. Remember that the benefit of the Four Quadrant model is balance. To function as a whole person requires that we develop the singular potential of each quadrant, and then integrate and balance all four. According to this model, we can then live a healthy holistic life. For example, to sit and read a book is using our mind, our intellect, and when we arrange our body in a supportive and comfortable seat then our intellectual and physical quadrants are working together. Our posture will allow our mind to be alert and efficient. When we feel sad and chant a Hindu mantra, our emotional quadrant and our spiritual quadrant support each other. Our sadness finds expression and comfort in an ancient spiritual practice. And so on. The Spiritual Practice at the end of this chapter can create ways to bring more balance.

If we are fortunate enough to have spiritual conversations, with ourselves, family members and others, they can be valuable and illuminative. We can be affirmed and celebrated for having the courage to ponder spiritual concerns, and we can more fully develop our spiritual quadrants. These days more than ever, we have access to the writings of women and men who have considered these questions down through the ages. With which of their writings do we resonate? Are our sources original texts or are they interpretations? We can create access to, and conversations with, the true mystics, then and now. The doors of the ancient libraries and monasteries have been flung open to us to use for our education and transformation. What does that mean for us, for our unfolding life, here and now? We become aware that others have asked these questions, and sought answers. We realize that spiritual seekers have always existed, have always asked such questions, and that they can become companions for our own spiritual journey. When, as a child, we are not able to have spiritual conversations, a wound is created. If family and friends refuse to engage with our spiritual questions, and criticize us for asking them, or judge us for not agreeing with their spiritual or religious beliefs, we suffer wounds. The result is confusion, a lack of fulfillment and often a feeling of being alone and empty.

The spiritual quadrant is the one to which the other three quadrants lead. Each of us was without form originally, 'a gleam in our parents' eyes'. When we die we return to spirit form. We may, or may not, believe in reincarnation or indeed anything after death. But all of us, even children, know people who have died. We have memories of them, especially people who had a significant impact on us, for good or ill. We can bring them, and their influences, to mind and into our hearts easily. Sometimes they come unbidden. What or who *is* that in our mind and in our heart? Yes, we have a memory of a particular quality: the image of a face, the feel of a touch, perhaps a smell, or hearing a tone of voice. These impressions are memories, to be sure, and are they not also a person in spirit form? This is the quadrant that can't be proven or demonstrated like the other quadrants. Yet what is unseen is no less real. The spiritual is the last, or the first, of these

Four Quadrants. It is as much a part of us as any of the other three, and to be a healthy person, in balance, the spiritual quadrant too needs to be acknowledged and expressed. (See the Spiritual Practices at the end of each chapter, and Chapter 8.)

While every person has a spirit, only some people express this by participating in spiritual practices or religious activity. Religion is more social: we may go to church, a mosque or a synagogue, join a coven, engage in rituals, read scriptures, go to baked bean suppers, sing hymns in congregation, pray together. Spirituality, however, is often quite private. I remember leading the first meeting of a group of people seeking more support and expression for their spiritual lives. We were going around the circle of about nine people, introducing ourselves, and we came to a woman who was barely in the room. She had been the last to arrive and was sitting in the doorway. She looked around and laughed, saying, "Where I'm sitting is no accident. I'm shy about my spiritual life." When our spiritual life is encouraged, it flowers and grows to be an equal partner with the other quadrants, thus creating the healthy balance we need. The result is the gift of inner peace.

Spiritual Practice: "Balanced"

Allow yourself to stand with your body straight and tall, secured by a strong foundation of firmly planted feet. This is the Yoga position of Mountain Pose, a posture of body prayer; standing tall, with your arms at your side, breathe into your whole form, taking the energizing air from the Universe into your lungs and then throughout your whole body. Slowly raise your arms and sweep them up until they point straight overhead. Feel the space you inhabit as a physical being: this is yours, the space to stand tall. Take a stand, have your place, exist here and now. Now notice how you feel, your natural emotion standing here. This is your emotional being, alive, well, conscious and expressing itself. Perhaps you feel peaceful. Now notice your mind observing and making sense of this body prayer. Now notice your lightness of being, your spirit. Feel your spirit embodied in your physical form, and also your energy body extending all around you for a few feet in every direction. Standing here, allow yourself to experience your wholeness and balance, the health of yourself, right now, in this space and time. You are living all Four Quadrants, now as one, because you stand in balance, aware, integrated, and embodying your physical, emotional, intellectual and spiritual self, whole.

Chapter 2

Emotional Path to Spirit

Meditation:
I feel excited: I sit.
I feel depressed: I sit.
I feel happy: I sit.
I feel sad: I sit.
Now I just sit.

Now let's look in more depth at the emotional quadrant, and investigate each natural emotion. First, it is key to understand that having feelings is natural. We have feelings as a natural consequence of being alive, of relating to and responding to our selves and the world around us. We feel because we are human; we are human because we feel. Our feelings are natural – native to us – an integral part of who we are as human beings. We have them for a reason: feelings have purposes. Each and every feeling has a specific reason for existing, a very positive use and benefit. This was not the message most of us received from our parents, our schools and our Western society! But over time, as our feelings come and go, they offer us gifts that allow us to know ourselves better and better.

A New Name
When my first marriage ended, I was consumed by feelings of sadness, relief and confusion. I rented an old house on a Maine island, reached by a narrow causeway that would flood after a combination of heavy rain and high tide. The solitude and beauty afforded me space and time to feel my feelings and soothe my aching soul. I felt I was a failure. I didn't know what to do. I was afraid the end of the marriage would damage my young daughter.

I didn't know how to be a single father to her. I walked the sandy beaches, and soaked in the peace and quiet, and let my feelings be. The solitary footprints I left in the sand washed away and were gone the next day. When I walked in the fresh sand I felt renewed. But weeks later when I took a teaching job at a small, alternative residential school miles away, I felt lost and unsure again, not knowing who I was or why I was going back to teaching. I drove up for the opening day to meet the new students. Amidst all the moving in, I welcomed a teenage girl and introduced myself, "Hi, my name is Dick Watson." She stood there in front of me, and looked me calmly in the eye. "No, it's not," she said. I was flustered, but went along with what I thought was her humor. But she wasn't smiling. So I said, "Well, what *is* my name?" She thought for a second, continued to look me in the eye, and then said, "Jacob." The rest of the term this was our private joke. When we saw each other around school, she'd call me Jacob. After a while, as I became more comfortable at the school, and in my new single life, I also became more comfortable with the name Jacob. I was coming out of the painful transitions of the last several years, more ready to let go of my marriage and who I had been. The chaos of feelings subsided as I acknowledged them, and I welcomed the student's new name for me as descriptive of my new self. I experimented by sending away for catalogs, and put 'Jacob' on the return address, so that several weeks later I'd get a catalog in the mail addressed to 'Jacob'. I'd stand on the front porch and look at the name I saw on the catalog I'd just taken out of the mailbox. Soon, I was telling my friends that I was using a new name, thus telling them I'd changed. Over the next few years, I became Jacob. Eventually I went back to the Bible and read the story of Jacob wrestling with the angel. I resonated with Jacob sustaining a wound, and with his all-night struggle with God. I now look back on that time of my life and recognize the value of letting go of an old identity, and the symbolic value of taking on a new name that personified my changes. Now I also see that names and nicknames are part of our egoic selves, and there is a nameless, universal me that doesn't need or have a name. This is the person who has feelings, but isn't defined by his or her feelings. Likewise, while I may have a new name, my essence is not defined by a name; it is nameless, formless and enduring.

Awareness

Our culture tells us some feelings are better to feel, easier to experience, and more pleasant than others. I was learning that every feeling is just a feeling. While we feel our feelings, sometimes very strongly, sometimes for a long time, *we are not our feelings.* We are humans *experiencing* our feelings, feelings that give us a full range of appropriate responses to survive and thrive in the world. Our five senses, sight, touch, smell, taste and hearing, and our all-important sixth sense, intuition, combine to flood our brain with information, which we need to live. Feelings result. But because the brain is fully enclosed in the hard shell of our skull, it is our mind – our consciousness – that interprets all this information. And our mind can understand, as Kübler-Ross taught, that the purpose of emotions is to open the heart, to feel the natural emotions, and thus to open the soul. Everything is moving and flowing to open the soul.

Being aware and conscious of our natural feelings, and expressing them, I believe, clears out pathways to the spiritual realm. Fritz Perls, the Gestalt therapist, said that awareness in and of itself is curative (see Chapter 7). How awareness promotes the development of meaning, even in an age of advanced science, is still being explored. But we *know* we are conscious beings, unique in all creation, and we know that we feel our feelings. Of course we like particular feelings, and dislike others. Not the point. We feel what we feel. There is no formula for what we ought to feel, or when we should feel it, though our culture has lots of prescriptions. But, over and over, we just feel what we feel. The key to health is to allow our feelings, that is, to be aware and conscious of what we are feeling, and to accept what we are feeling. As this happens we can then find a way, a safe, non-hurtful way (to our self and to others), to give these feelings expression, to put outside what was inside. Relief, meaning and perspective result.

Externalization

To give our natural emotions life is to give them expression or externalization, a word coined by Elisabeth Kübler-Ross. But this isn't enough. Yes, to express feelings helps us cope with this world. But this life – at least a fulfilled life – is not simply about coping; this life is more than just getting through the day, or the night. To be fully human is to reach our full potential, to find and live our essence. When we have the courage to express our emotional truth, in the precious present moment, which is all we have, not only do we live a more healthy and balanced life, we transform ourselves. Externalization is transformation: letting our suffering out. When we share it with another human being we are no longer alone. When we share and connect, we become the artist of our own change, healing and transformation. Externalization can transform pain and suffering into relief and beauty. Andrew Harvey once said in a class, "You will be graced with the necessary catastrophes; they will take away your hiding places and reveal unbelievable beauty." Life's catastrophes bring a full range of natural emotions: I'm sad. I'm in love. (Yes, this is sometimes a catastrophe!) I'm afraid. I'm angry. I'm grieving. Then what? Each and every feeling will arise and pass away, and as it does, it accomplishes its clearing work. When we can take a step back and witness this coming and going, we can see the beauty underneath, the essence. The keening of a bereaved mother has a haunting beauty about it. A songwriter's images of loss transform the expressed emotions into artistry: the solace of song.

All artists, including the artist inside us, can show us the way to express our feelings, and thus our spirit or soul. Writers, poets, singers and songwriters use words and melodies to express feelings. Sometimes words can't describe what we feel: there are no words, or there are too many words. Then music, paint, photography, writing, dance, fabric or clay become the medium for expression, for externalization and thus for healing and growth into the next realm. (See Chapter 13.)

If you bring forth what is within you,
What you bring forth will save you.
If you do not bring forth what is within you,
What you do not bring forth will destroy you.
– The Gnostic Gospels

Uninvited Guests

When, for whatever reason, and there are good ones, especially as we grow up and have to survive in a family system, we choose not to express our natural emotions, they do not just fade away peacefully into oblivion. Even when we consciously, sometimes desperately, push feelings away, they retain a life, energy. When feelings are repressed over time, they build up and collect in our unconscious. They simmer, they brood, they fester and they drain energy away from the present. Unexpressed feelings take up space in our psyche, get distorted, and, worst of all, they distort and grow bigger. They hang around wanting only one thing: acknowledgement and expression. If feelings don't get opportunities for expression, they will create them. If feelings aren't invited out, they will invite themselves out. They will bubble or burst forth, and usually not when we want them to! They are like uninvited guests, hiding in the closet, covered with cobwebs, mumbling words that drip with threats of chaos and ruin. All these feelings want is expression, their moment in the sun, externalization. It's much better when we are proactive and let them out; we can offer them space and time for expression when we're ready for them. To make the choice to express feelings is a new kind of relief and freedom. Contrary to the message of our culture, we do not always have to know *why* we are feeling what we feel. Our culture sends us the message that if we can find the cause of the suffering and then somehow fix it, all will be OK. But if we focus too much on the 'why', then we move from our emotional quadrant to our intellectual quadrant, up into our head. The feeling slips away, unacknowledged and unexpressed. If we're convinced by the culture that we must know why we are feeling, for example, sad, then we can easily get lost and distracted. We will certainly have less access to the original natural emotion of sadness. And if we can't find a reason for it, then suddenly we may feel we've lost our right to feel the feeling. The truth is that we don't have to have a reason to feel any feeling, any natural emotion. We feel what we feel. Granted, sometimes it's interesting to know why we feel a feeling, *but it's not necessary.* What *is* necessary, for our emotional health and healing, is to allow whatever feeling we are experiencing to have an outlet, a way out of our system, an expression. As we allow this movement of emotion to happen, because it wants to happen, we are expressing our spirit, our essence. This is our authentic self, transformed by the person consumed by emotion into a person conscious of a deeper self.

Emotions as Spirit

Our emotions are often the first fragile and tender seedlings of self-awareness and self-expression. It is easy to appreciate this in a child. When a little boy or girl has strong feelings, he or she doesn't yet have the intellect to explain or subdue their feelings: they just come out. Whether it's a temper tantrum in the vegetable section of the supermarket, or screaming at Granny's holiday dinner table, out the feelings come. The child, in that moment, is expressing his or her spirit. Eventually, as children become socialized, they will learn what and when is 'appropriate' regarding the expression of their feelings, and there are benefits to that. It's easier to get along in a big world. Sometimes, children learn inappropriate expressions of feelings from their role models. But in either case, they also must learn that their feelings, their natural emotions, are just that: natural. Hopefully, as we grow up we will learn that every feeling has a purpose and that our feelings are precious. Indeed, they make us unique. This is the work we will plunge into in the following chapters as we investigate the purposes of each emotion – our natural responses to being human – and how they provide pathways to spirit.

When the cold and hardened sorrows of our soul start to melt, like ice that is exposed to the heat of the sun, our natural emotions, our human feelings, touch us so that we can begin to join the watery play of the creative life force itself. The energies of the heart are like a mighty river. The ocean awaits.

Spiritual Practice: "Clearing and Cleaning"

Find a time and place to sit comfortably. Bring your feelings. Breathe in and out so that you trust your physical self to care for you in this moment, to provide you with what you need. Remind yourself that here you do not have to use your intellect, your intellectual quadrant, to solve any problems. You can let yourself be as you are in this moment. Now allow yourself to feel whatever it is that you feel, an emotion, a feeling in your heart or your gut. Any feeling will do, even if you can't name it. And feeling 'nothing' counts too. No judgment about liking or disliking what comes. Know that this feeling, whatever it is, is uniquely yours in this moment. No one else is feeling quite this emotion at this time and place. The feeling is so intense that you might believe that the feeling defines who you are, but now you understand that you are a human being experiencing this feeling. You gain a small distance so you can be a witness to the feeling. Even this intimate feeling will come and go, clearing a pathway to your spirit, your essence. Remember, it's not that you have to do anything here, except to welcome your emotion into your awareness, as it does its cleaning work.

Chapter 3

Grief: Letting Go

Meditation:
As we sit in the silence, we breathe out, we breathe in.
Breathing out at the end of the breath we have the opportunity to
experience our death. Now we breathe in, continuing life, yet
practicing, practicing for that inevitable one time we won't.

Now we will look deeply into each of the Natural Emotions, beginning with grief. Grief is a natural response to life's losses. It precipitates sadness, often expressed by our tears, and eventually encourages us to share our stories with other people. When we put grief into words it is a creative act, a primary way to both say our truth about our losses out loud, and to connect with others. To feel and express the natural emotion of grief is like hauling up a bucket of water from a dark well into the sunlight. Eventually we can use the water to nurture the growth of new life.

As we live, we have inevitable losses, so we respond to them: we think, we feel, and we act. We do not simply have life, or do life: we *are* life. Built into this is, of course, death. We are death, too. We learn that all the stories of life come and go. If we were 'not alive' once, we will be 'not alive' again. Because of this natural cycle, we will have loss, and thus we will experience grief. As soon as we enter the natural cycle of life, we begin grieving. (See Meditation Prayer in Chapter 12.) Every day of life brings transition and loss. Some are small and inconsequential. Even to climb out of a warm, cozy bed in winter, or to leave one room to enter another, are losses. We put one foot in front of the other and step forward, leaving behind our footprint where we used to stand. When we shift our gaze from one object of sight to another it involves moving our eyes away from something, leaving something, in order to fasten our gaze on the new object. Life brings much larger losses, such as the end of a relationship, the transition from a job, the deterioration of health, aging, or the death of a friend or family member. Whenever we begin to love we begin to grieve. We grieve first because of the possibility of change, when the grief is anticipatory. Then the change happens, sometimes expected, and sometimes shocking and unexpected. Either way, we learn that to have is to create the surety of not having, of losing, and when we experience loss, we grieve. To be human means we are bound to feel the natural emotion of grief.

Purpose of Grief

Like each of the Natural Emotions, grief has a purpose, and the purpose of grief is to learn to live with life's losses. Another purpose of grief is to open our hearts to the losses of other people and thus to activate our compassion. Some grief we feel and live with alone, and eventually, as part of the grieving process, we share it. In the moment when we have the courage to walk through a door, sit down next to or across from other people, and say out loud what our loss is, the fact, and how we feel – the emotion itself – we begin to heal. Most of the time, but not always, it is helpful to express out loud what and how it happened – share the story. Telling our story, our felt experience of it, can be a major step into and through our grief towards healing. While we heal, to understand that grief has a purpose can be comforting. When the grief is fierce and unrelenting, which it certainly can be, to know that grief is purposeful, that it has both meaning and use, is normalizing, humanizing and, eventually, healing. I have had occasions to say to grieving families who feel overwhelmed by their grief, "No, you are not crazy, you are grieving." Grief has its own process and time line, and, similar to the other Natural Emotions, grief seeks acknowledgement and expression.

The Black Schooner

At age 93 my dad's health had been slowly failing. He was content to sit in his worn red leather chair, eyes closed. But we had to watch out, we couldn't count on him being asleep, and often we were caught by surprise saying something and he'd come up out from his supposed slumber and answer us, as if he'd been in the conversation all along. His health had been deteriorating for several months when I received a phone call from my sister saying he was fading and I should come down. I was about 15 minutes away when my sister called me in my car to say that he had died. When I arrived I went right to his bedroom. Dad was lying on his back. His mouth was open, not too differently from when he'd go to sleep in his red leather chair in the living room. But this was different. He was different, no longer there. I sat down in a chair by his bed and took his hand, which was still warm, though just barely. My sister was in and out. I looked at this man who was my father, who had been my father all these many years. I began to cry for all he had given me, and all that he had not given me. It was over. The room was quiet. He looked as if he were asleep. It did indeed feel like all the recent years when he would sleep in his chair, with the noises of the house around him but not disturbing his peace. Now his peace was forever. I looked up and out the window at the harbor that he so deeply loved, the harbor where he had kept his beloved catboat when he was a young man, and later his little motorboats, as his father had before him. Out of the corner of my eye, I saw something moving across the harbor and looked more closely, still holding my father's hand. There in the channel heading out of the harbor was the big black schooner, Tabor Boy. All her sails, two jibs, the mainsail and her topsails, were hoisted, unusual inside the harbor, and she was gathering speed, headed out the entranceway into the bay. My dad had sailed on the Tabor Boy to Bermuda once, and he loved the old ship. I felt his spirit, now free, sail along with the black schooner out of the harbor into open water with the ocean beyond. I stayed with Dad's body all night sitting in the chair at the foot of his bed. I was content to join him in his peace, to accompany him through the night, as he had accompanied me for so many years. In the deep part of the night, when the room was lit only by the flickering votive candle on Dad's bedside table, I cried more tears. They expressed again the finality of his death, his love for me, and despite our differences, how much we shared, being little boys, being men. Mostly I felt gratitude.

Losing Jenny

When my sister Lea's partner Jenny died of cancer in California, Lea grieved deeply. Our family flew out for the memorial service that we created in the Redwood Park across from their home where Jenny and Lea used to hike. In the quiet glade surrounded by the ancient and stately redwood trees, we remembered Jenny in stories, poems and songs. Several months later, Lea began to feel a pull to go back into her sculpture studio. But her grief was pervasive, unrelenting and tiring. Yet the urge persisted. Finally she found the energy to get out some clay and work with it, to get her hands back into the earth and water, the mud of her grief. Soon, a grieving figure emerged on her workbench, body stretched out in grief, hands raised. Some days later another figure came out of the clay, this one bent over, collapsed inward in anguish. Again and again, over time, grieving figures emerged from the clay. Lea told me that she would stand in front of her pottery bench, and allow her feelings of grief to arise, then let her own body take the form of the feeling; the body position arose from the feeling. Then she'd put her hands into the wet clay and let the form appear. After Lea glazed and fired the figures, almost twenty of them, she placed them all over her house. You could not go anywhere in her home without encountering grief, expressed in a clay figure. They were in the living room, the bathroom, closets, the kitchen, outside on the porch, in the garden. Anyone who visited her house saw Lea's grief manifested, tangible, alive, expressed. Her suffering was transformed into a true and harsh beauty, into works of powerful and graceful art, powerful evidence of her healing. As the months, then years unfolded following Jenny's death, some of the statues disappeared, one by one. But there is always one somewhere in Lea's house, just as there is, somewhere in Lea's heart, some trace of her grief over losing Jenny.

Distortions of Grief

If the natural feeling of grief is not expressed for weeks and years, it becomes distorted into blame, guilt, and shame. Distorted means that it becomes outsized and toxic. Now, it must be said that sometimes we *are* victimized. But the whole point of recognizing the distortions of Natural Emotions is not to remain stuck as a victim. Yes, when we feel victimized, we want to find other people to blame. It seems as if what happened to us, the loss, is someone else's fault. We want to blame the other person, the drunken driver, the doctor who diagnosed us with cancer, or the cancer disease itself. Sometimes we blame ourselves: we should have done something differently, protected our loved one, or simply treated him better, or told her we loved her. With knowledge of this process, we can be alerted when the distortions of blame, guilt, and victimization show up. Yes, there is blame, and responsibility. Yet all the screaming and ranting when we blame a perpetrator, while cathartic, never takes away the grief. Our acts of blame possibly can increase vulnerability and violence. Safety is paramount; we must not increase the likelihood of more violence or hurt, or take actions that might produce additional grief for others or ourselves. After blame comes the responsibility to regain control over what we can, and then we can work with our grief.

Another distortion of grief is guilt. We might feel guilty for all we meant to do for a sick friend, but somehow never quite got around to doing it. We can feel guilty for feeling less – or more – grief than is acceptable to our friends and family, or to ourselves. Having regrets can bring guilt. But this guilt is a distortion of grief. When we are feeling guilty, we can ask what we might be angry about. Guilt can hide anger, so when we look more deeply into what we are feeling guilty about, we may find anger, with its clarity and energy (see Chapter 4). The key to healing grief is to return to feeling the natural emotion, and give it acknowledgement and expression.

Another distortion of grief is shame, perhaps the trickiest to work with. Shame is subtle and pervasive. We can be ashamed of what we are feeling. We expect, or we think others expect, different feelings than the ones we have. To move beyond shame we must remember that we have a right to our natural emotions. Our emotions help us accept and live with our losses. We can remember that our emotions have purposes. There is no reason to be ashamed of a human quality that is native to human beings. Take a good look at our shame. We may be able to see it for what it is: a wounded ego desperately trying to salvage itself at our expense. It is helpful to say the simple truth out loud, "I am sad." We can then recall the gratitude we feel for being able to acknowledge and express our natural emotions.

A Puppy Named Watch

When I was about ten years old we got a dog, a little beagle hound puppy. We named him Watch. He was sweet and cuddly, and when we sat down to eat supper at the end of the day, he would crawl under the kitchen table. He'd fall asleep with his little furry head resting on top of my shoe, the weight warming my foot. We'd had him for several weeks when one day he didn't come home in the afternoon. I was afraid and sad. We all went out to look for him. We walked the neighborhood calling for him, but we couldn't find him. And he wasn't waiting for us when we came back home. Dejected and worried, my parents, my sisters and I sat down at the kitchen table for supper, but we missed Watch and couldn't eat. I wanted to talk about my feelings about Watch: my fear and concern. Where was he? I felt guilty: I should have made sure he stayed in the yard. As I started to cry, and express my worry and fear, just then my parents got up from the table to clear away the dishes, and then make some phone call. I wanted to talk about my feelings but there was no one to listen. My sisters and I went out again to search for Watch. We walked into the tall bushes in back of the house, and called his name over and over. Eventually we had to come home and go to bed. Several days later we learned that Watch had been killed on the trolley tracks near our house. But my mother and father didn't show much sadness; we started to discuss what kind of dog we would get next. But I didn't want another dog. Deep inside I knew I hadn't grieved for Watch, that my sadness and tears were still unexpressed. I still missed him, especially the way he had put his little head on my shoe under the kitchen table. Somewhere inside me I felt a double loss, the loss of Watch and the loss of being able to express my sadness.

Losing Friends

Ten years after I helped my friend Bill start the Center for Grieving Children, he developed colon cancer. As his illness progressed, we would hang out with each other, and discuss the progress of the Center we both cared about so much. We shared our anticipatory grief with each other, knowing he was dying, even as we worked to support the grieving families who came to our center. He was quite sick the day he asked me to take him to the downtown space being renovated for the Center's first real home. I helped him walk slowly up the long and steep stairway to the main floor. It was littered with construction debris and noisy with electricians and carpenters hammering away. We had to step around holes in the floor, snaking wires, and pieces of sheetrock and trim boards. He loved it. He insisted on sitting right in the middle of all the chaos. Several months later, Bill died a few hours after the Center had moved into its new space. I felt that once Bill was assured the Center had a new home, he was free to leave, to die. A week later I was standing in front of a church full of grieving people saying, "I don't want to be here doing this. I'd much rather be at the deli eating crab cakes with Bill." I was sad and grieving. We all were sad and grieving, remembering Bill. In that sense, we were keeping him, or a part of him, with us. Bill helped that experience by recording a tape of his favorite songs that we played while people came into the church. The lyrics and melodies wrapped us in Bill's arms. We were enfolded in his love and spirit. I felt vulnerable showing my sadness in public, standing up there with tears on my face. I couldn't hide it, and I yet knew I was with Bill's friends and family, and we were all grieving. This sharing of my emotional truth was helpful in my own grieving process. Together, we told Bill stories, and expressed our collective gratitude for Bill's vision and courage to start the Center. As we grieved together, I experienced Bill's presence with us, now in a very different but palpable spiritual form. And because we were close friends and colleagues, he left something else with me, something powerful and pure, the passion to provide a safe place and a safe process to express the natural feeling of grief.

A few years later, only a few months after his diagnosis of lung cancer, my best friend Rick died several days after Christmas. When I received the sad telephone call from his wife, I drove out to his house in the country. After all my trips out to see him, this time the road looked different, not as familiar, the trip longer. I wanted the road to go on and on so that I never had to arrive. But I did arrive. I walked into their living room as I had many times before. Rick's body lay in a hospital bed, still, beside the family Christmas tree, which was decorated with lights and family ornaments. His wife and his four young sons ambled in and out, crying, sad, confused, shocked. We sat together. We talked. We were quiet. We looked at Rick. We didn't look at Rick. We touched him. We felt sad, awkward and loving. So sad. We said goodbye to Rick. Eventually we called the funeral home to come and pick up his body. When the van left with his body, we looked at the empty room, we looked at each other, and more tears came. The house had never felt so empty. Several weeks later, I was again standing in front of a church full of grieving people, to grieve again the death of a dear friend, this time officiating at Rick's funeral service. Rick's wife and their boys sat in the front row, and his many friends filled the sanctuary, the foyer and hallways outside. I felt my tears come. Later I realized that my natural feeling of grieving Rick's death eclipsed any distorted feelings of shame I had from crying in front of so many people. I had written out the service because I knew I would be feeling so much I probably wouldn't be able to remember everything I wanted to say. Again, it was soothing to acknowledge out loud what I was feeling, and to be with Rick's loving community. We were grieving together. I ended the memorial service by encouraging people to have a glass of good Merlot wine – his favorite – in honor of Rick, and to make a toast to him. We were recognizing that Rick, in very different form, was still a part of our lives. Again, I felt the precious and fragile spirit of a friend still with me, now part of my life in a new way. Instead of having to call my friends to arrange a lunch or hike together, now they are with me all the time.

Losing Bill and Rick was hard; two dear friends were taken way before their time, still relatively young men. What that word 'hard' means is that I *felt* a lot, a lot of sadness, a lot of grief. When we say, "Life is hard, or difficult," what we are saying is that life is full of feelings: grief and all our natural emotions. A healing strategy is to become aware of these distorted feelings and by accepting their existence we can move them into the present to express them. Indeed, the present is the only place that healing can happen. We can review and even revisit the past, but we cannot change it. At the other end of the spectrum, we can plan the future but not live there. The present moment is what we have to work with, to move our grief out of the distorted feelings of blame, guilt, shame and victimization. Then we can experience them in the present, appreciate their purpose and externalize them, express them out into the world. As we express the natural emotion of grief, we are expressing our spirit. The spiritual realms open up to us, never more so than in these examples of grieving dear friends who die to another world, while a part of their spirit – their essence – remains with us forever.

Spiritual Practice: "Lamentation"

Allow yourself a shroud of space, probably best late at night in the dark. Find a comfortable and private space. Center yourself by remembering that the earth supports you below, and the heavens are open to you above. Give yourself permission to lament, to bring forward in your awareness the natural feelings of your loss and grief. Let yourself feel how much and how deeply you feel what once was yours and now is no longer yours in physical form, the coming and the going, the having and the not having, the possessing and the losing, all the letting go. Your body will guide you, from initially sensing the foggy mists of sadness, the tremors, the changes brought by feelings waking up, then moving into expression. Tears may come. If you sense the feelings are building too much, you can slow and quiet your breath. Your grief will move and flow naturally like a stream finding its way through a meadow. Let your grief come up and out, quietly, then with some sound. Feel the wave build and then eventually recede. Allow yourself the ensuing calmness and peace.

Chapter 4

Anger: Dark Night of the Soul

Meditation:
Sitting, remember: just as the drama of ocean storms obscures the placid depths below the surface, so does human trauma hide the quiet depths of our soul.

The natural feeling of anger gives us powerful insight into our core energy, often quite suddenly. A burst of anger can illuminate a strong belief, a sudden and perhaps startling caring. A piece of our essence suddenly shines forth. Suddenly we feel our passion. Anger shows us what we care about, what we are willing to defend, or pursue. Anger is useful to object to injustice and to defend ourselves when necessary. It can give us the sudden adrenalin to protect ourselves in a life-threatening situation, to move us out of danger to safety.

Purpose of Anger

The purpose of anger is to help us change, to remind us of the energy we have inside us, and to use that energy to rally ourselves to take a stand, sometimes literally, to stand up, to speak up and express our passion. We all experience everyday anger and annoyance. We may not like angry feelings, but as author and therapist Miriam Greenspan says, "The dark emotions are purposeful." If we can acknowledge angry feelings in the moment, express them safely, they will serve their purpose to wake us up, fuel change and give us their gift of energy. Then they will pass, melt away and disappear. However, if we can't or don't acknowledge and release angry feelings, they will accumulate, build up over time and eventually solidify into hate and rage. This is when and how unexpressed anger becomes debilitating, and possibly dangerous, when it drains us of clarity and energy, and even becomes a threat to ourselves and those around us. It takes enormous energy to repress the natural feeling of anger, to overlook it, or pretend we're not bothered, not angry. When we have the courage to admit we're angry about something, when we become aware of it, that consciousness releases energy that we can use to express the anger.

The benefit of expressing anger is true across cultures, though how one does it needs to be consistent with the social mores of each culture. Otherwise more anger will be generated. Respect is called for. I have found that teaching safe anger externalization to people around the United States, including Alaska, and also overseas in South Korea, England and Scotland, is helpful to their healing. Each of these cultures has their own way of avoiding and repressing natural emotions, often in the context of their families: people do not want to upset their parents and children. Asian cultures especially hold their parents, grand-parents and other family members in such reverent esteem and honor that the expression of anger to or about them is not openly permitted. When I offered Korean Hospice professionals and volunteers the opportunity to express their anger, they giggled nervously. It was inconceivable to them to show strong emotions about their family unless and until they were assured of complete privacy and confidentiality. They would and did express anger at peers, sometimes at doctors, but seldom at family members. Because of this cultural value of respect for their elders, these workshop participants did not hold on to their anger as long and therefore usually avoided a build-up into hate and rage.

Scotland Workshop

The warden of a maximum-security prison in Scotland had heard about the Kübler-Ross five-day Life, Death and Transition workshops, and I knew she had an interest in taking them into prisons. He and Elisabeth negotiated for over a year. Elisabeth insisted that the workshop participants be made up of a mixture of prison inmates, both men and women, and prison staff members. The warden feared this mixture would be too volatile. Inmates were usually strictly segregated by gender, and staff and inmates met only under very limited and proscribed restrictions. But Elisabeth, true to her principles, persisted. She knew that inmates and staff alike would have their share of natural emotions from their life histories, criminal or not. In fact, to share their stories together could offer profound healing. The workshop was held inside the prison, where our staff lived for the week. The minute we walked in, I heard and felt the anger in the prison. Everything was steel and stone. The gray steel bars and locks only seemed to amplify the anger, not control it. The PA system growled instructions, rules and schedules. Everything seemed loud: the public address system, the clicking locks, the profane language, the clanging of steel furniture and closing of metals bars and doors. It even smelled loud. Yet, when we began the workshop, all the participants held to the rules of safety and confidentiality we established. After we taught the basic idea of Natural Emotions and the need to express them, we offered participants, one at a time, the tools and the opportunity to physically express anger: rubber hoses to smash up old telephone books. Person after person – inmate or guard or administrator – trudged up to the front of the room and took a turn. The whole group sat around the prisoner or the guard – whoever was sharing at the time – and witnessed horrible and touching stories. As the tales poured out: physical and sexual abuse, alcoholism, injury, beatings, illness and death, along with the deprivation and isolation of incarceration, we staff and participants provided support and encouragement. The person working cried, screamed and raged. Despite the earlier fears of the prison staff, everyone followed our rules and stayed on the workshop mattress. Later, participants continued their externalization work in smaller back rooms, with our staff facilitating. Only once, a participant didn't quite make it to the back room, and out of anger he punched a hole in the hallway wall. He kept going down the hall, and finished his anger expression using our tools. But he didn't punch a person. As the workshop progressed, it became clear that everyone, whether inmate or staff, had lots of unfinished business to work on, heartbreaking stories to share and natural feelings, especially anger, to express. Elisabeth knew well that both inmates and staff alike had suffered loss, and needed to tell their stories and do the work of externalizing their emotions. Many inmates were in prison for long sentences. The staff: guards, social workers, psychologists, and administrators could leave the prison at the end of their workday, but they carried their own prisons around with them. To live with unexpressed emotions is to live in a prison. At the end of the workshop, we all shared one last meal together, our Kübler-Ross staff, prison inmates and staff, including the wardens. A Scottish bagpiper honored my colleagues and me by playing his pipes as we entered the prison dining hall. The inmates and staff stood and applauded us, and we in turn applauded them. Tears came to my eyes and ran down my face. I felt the common bond that had been created when we witnessed the participants' emotional stories: the feelings of anger, sadness, fear and love, and their spirits that would not be extinguished by time inside steel and stone. Later, we walked out of the prison gate to leave, and the inmates showed us what they had planted and maintain in the main courtyard. Against the high gray walls of the prison behind them, little red and yellow flowers lifted their heads. I walked away from the inmates through the last steel gate, and turned to wave goodbye. I felt a surge of sadness as I watched them bravely wave back. I left behind in the prison people I now knew intimately. I took with me a new realization of the ways I imprison myself, the humble understanding of our similarities. The next several years our staff provided follow-up workshops because workshop participants asked for additional opportunities to work. The inmates' and the staff's courage to work to heal themselves changed me. I was inspired by their willingness to reveal, under their deep wounds, the radiance and magnificence that is still alive.

Distortions of Anger

Among the many distortions of anger are hate, rage and depression. Hate and rage result from everyday annoyances and angers being ignored over long periods of time. Without opportunities for expression, the feelings build up, fester and become poisonous. The idea that depression is anger turned inward has some merit. But any feeling not expressed can lead to depression. The critical point here is to let go of whichever feeling we experience and find a way to express it. In Western culture, we are taught to ignore or suppress any feeling we don't like, or that we think would make other people, especially family, uncomfortable. But the feeling, especially anger, just goes underground, into our unconscious; we can become unconscious of having ever felt the emotion in the first place. Sometimes when the emotion is strong enough, we even suppress the memory of the event that precipitated the emotion. This is called dissociation. In denying feelings, there is no filter: when we suppress a feeling we might not like, we suppress all feelings. When we suppress anger, we also suppress joy; when we suppress grief, we also suppress ecstasy. As we heal, we become able to express our natural emotions because we have the courage to express *any* natural emotion – especially the ones with which we might not be comfortable. When we express our anger we have access to our joy. When we express our sadness we have access to our ecstasy. This allows us to acknowledge, feel and express the full range of human emotion, and therefore to live as fully expressive and realized human beings, human beings with spirit.

The Nice Guy

The news media brings us examples of an individual who 'snaps' and commits murder. His neighbors, interviewed, describe the perpetrator as a 'nice guy'. "He helped me take out my trash every week." Maybe so, but there was a probability that he was sitting on years of unexpressed anger that had turned into rage, and suddenly it was triggered and burst forth, with tragic results. The lesson? Find safe ways to keep your anger moving (see Chapter 7, Gestalt Awareness Cycle) so that the natural small angers get expressed safely and don't build up into hate and rage. We can use the clarity that anger can bring to focus, to energize, to accomplish a task, to make a statement, to act in service to others.

When I feel angry and despairing, a loving God or Spirit seems far away, inattentive and unresponsive to my suffering. I am being asked to grimace and bear it. I have learned that God or Spirit is in the suffering, with me, holding me, attending me. While I wait the suffering out, it waits for me to let it out. I can let the anger out, let the currents of anger wash over me and through me. This is as natural as the ocean tides that ebb and flow to create currents. My sailing experience has taught me that the currents run strongest, the waves are most dangerous, in the constricted channels, the tight places. And all this time, the ocean lies stretched out there beyond the rocks and headlands, broad, expansive and capable of holding all the waves in the world.

Ripping Up Phone Books

In addition to the Kübler-Ross workshops mentioned above, I have facilitated other workshops where anger is expressed physically at the Center for Grieving Children and the Chaplaincy Institute of Maine. Circles of staff members, volunteers or students gather to learn the purpose of safely expressing anger, and then do it for themselves. Safe expression demands careful facilitation; anger and rage are powerful emotions. The physical environment must be safe, contained, and soundproof, with no hard edges of furniture anywhere, and with lots of pillows and mattresses. The emotional environment must be safe and confidential, led by trained facilitators who have done their own externalization work. They provide acceptance and love: no judgments or comments, however well intentioned, and no interruptions. The spiritual environment must be safe: no agendas about what God should or shouldn't have done, no platitudes such as "God has a plan that includes death."

Typically I pass around old telephone books, emphasize the safety guidelines I described above, and also stipulate no throwing books or criticizing anyone in any way. Participants do not need to come up with words, rational explanations, or justifications for their feelings. They just need the courage to pick up the telephone book and begin tearing it up. Everyone generally stays in silence to facilitate the personal experience and avoid distractions. No one witnessing need express either encouragement or judgment: this is an intimate, revealing and courageous act that requires each person to use his or her own energy. Importantly, I state that I will clean up after the process; no one has to muck around in his or her own crap after they've expressed it. Both kids and adults like this particular guideline! Once I experienced an objection to my offer to clean up. I had been working with an eleven-year-old boy who had lost his father. In my home office he raged and raged, yelling and smashing old telephone books to pieces. After he finished and I began picking up the torn pages, he stopped me and said, "I want to show my mom." So together we gathered up all the ripped up pages and put them in a big black trash bag. I watched out my window as he walked out to meet his mother, and proudly held up the bag to show her what he had accomplished. I learned another lesson in the value of deep emotional expressive work: the 'bag of gold'. He was celebrating his accomplishment and the freedom he now felt: "Here's all my work, and now I can let it go."

As participants throw the torn telephone book or newspaper pages into the center of the circle, the mood in the circle changes. The pile of ripped paper in the middle of the circle grows, and participants have the visceral and visual experience to see right in front of them the real and symbolic anger they have been carrying around and living with. A sense of relief arises around the circle. Faces look different. The mood is lighter. People acknowledge their transformation by breathing easier, even laughing as they feel a new sense of freedom. It is important to allow some time afterwards to share out loud what the experience brought up for each group member, so they can affirm and normalize their expression of anger. Participants usually feel a growing confidence that, having done this once, they will be able to do it again: now they have the tools to create a safe environment in which to express and externalize their natural anger, and do so before it turns to hate and rage. The exact scenario may change somewhat: some people like to yell at the ocean waves, or at trees in a forest, or rip up newspapers at home in private. But the gift to ourselves of creating – and it is a creative act – a safe and effective method of being able to move anger, to externalize rage and hate – to lighten up – is profoundly healing and transformative, literally enlightening.

Spiritual Practice: "Releasing Anger"

To do this, give yourself time and space to feel your anger and rage, the dark emotions of your hidden spirit. Prepare mindfully. Build in whatever safety you need, such as setting a kitchen timer for five or ten minutes to feel anger. It might work best to choose a time at night, when it is literally dark outside, to mirror your darkness inside. You'll need a private physical space – even if it's just a corner of your living room – and time without interruption. Find an old telephone book or some newspapers that you don't want anymore, and a trash bag, and have them available. Sit in silence to center yourself, and then give yourself permission to feel some of your unexpressed anger and rage. Breathe your feelings out into expression and externalization. Put outside what has been inside for so long. If you want to close your eyes, do so. Now bring the feelings up from your gut and chest and out your arms and hands and fingers. Pick up some paper and rip it up. Tear the paper up however you want to: into small little strips or big half-pages. Let images come, of events or people about whom you feel anger. Forget any need to know *why* you feel anger, just express it. If words come, speak them out loud while you rip. Continue until you're finished feeling angry, for now. Stop when the kitchen timer goes off. Rest. Now look in front of you at the torn paper. You have been carrying all that around inside you, and now it is outside you. It's not all your anger, but it's part of your anger. And you have externalized, released it. You can do it again, when you need to. When you are ready, pick up the torn paper and put it into the trash bag, and know this is the last time you will have to handle this piece of old anger. Put the bag in the recycling bin, and feel your new lightness and freedom.

Chapter 5

Fear: Contraction

Meditation:
Silence is not the absence of noise; it is the sound of your soul.

Life at times can be dangerous. The natural emotion of fear provides us with a valuable tool to protect ourselves when necessary. There are times to contract, to curl up and make ourselves small, to hibernate and shut the world out. This can be a time of protection, rest and renewal. Fear is useful to get our attention and to alert us to danger. It is crucial, even lifesaving, to listen to fear, to hear what it is telling us, to respond to a threat – to move, to contract, to defend ourselves, to get out of the way. Fear, like anger, is also useful for giving us the energy to take a stand, to plant both feet on the ground, to harvest the immediate support and energy of Mother Earth. We can shelter ourselves when necessary – there will be times we must do that – to protect our physical and emotional beings. Yet while these survival skills are necessary to employ when needed, this is no way to live a life: small, contracted, defended, in fear.

The Divine does not want us to shrink beyond measure, to make ourselves invisible. This is not how we are called by the Divine to live, not how we are part of Creation. After the storm, when we have survived the threat, or perhaps simply after we have had a chance to rest, it is time to re-emerge, to re-energize and move ahead, to step out into the world. Like the smallest expression of nature, we are encouraged to grow into our fullness, to join with the fullness of the Universe. A primary way to expand is to enter a state of acceptance and gratitude, to feel and join with the abundance around us. Often going outdoors to be in nature helps. We can thank Creation and its many expressions for the precious privilege of being alive here at this time, in physical form, in body and in spirit.

Purpose of Fear

The purpose of fear is caution. Fear is a healthy response to the threats in the environment around us. When I get in my car after a winter snowstorm, drive down the street and I see that the surface of the road is icy, I sometimes feel a clutch of fear in my chest. My fear tells me to slow down. That fear is purposeful and could be lifesaving. However, if I become obsessed with the fear that I'll have a car accident in the winter, the natural healthy emotion has become locked into place over time. It no longer serves me, at least if I want to live in a snowy place like Maine.

Families who have suffered a loss may know they are grieving – they feel their sadness – but they don't like to feel the fear; they want to get rid of their fearful feelings. They are afraid of the fragility of their family, the strength of their anxiety. What misfortune might come next? They are often afraid of very practical things. They worry about who will shop for food, how will family meals go, especially holiday gatherings and family anniversaries such as births and future losses. Should we leave her chair at the kitchen table, or put it away? What do we say to well-meaning friends who ask how we are doing? How *are* we doing? Should I see a counselor, take medication? Will I ever be able to sleep through the night again? What will my life be without him? And then come the spiritual questions: Why did this death happen to me, to my family? Does God care about us? What will give my life meaning and security now that my partner is gone? What use is it to pray to God? After feeling all this fear, will I ever feel safe again?

To ask these questions is a good way to begin to express fears. To investigate these fears instead of ignoring them or pretending they don't exist is purposeful. These are questions without easy answers; they must be lived into. The search is valuable and provides meaning and direction. I remind families that some fear is useful, helpful and healthy. Again, it comes down to awareness of what we feel, and allowing it to come up and out. Without externalizing our fear, it languishes inside; it keeps us contracted – even paralyzed – and, subsequently, it keeps us alone. Fear, both acknowledged and unacknowledged, can debilitate us and immobilize us. Like the other natural emotions, what fear seeks is expression. We can acknowledge that we feel fear, and then find some way to express it out loud. We can say the words, "I'm afraid." This may mean we let go of our expectations – and others' expectations of us – such as being fearless, of being the 'rock' of the family. We often want to play an old role, to be 'cool' or unafraid or courageous. We may be trapped in old prescriptions, patterns and roles (see Chapter 8: Living Our Essence). To feel fear may not fit with our self-image, or how we wish to be seen by our family and friends. But fear, like the other natural emotions, cannot be willed away. Indeed it has a profoundly valuable purpose. Fear is deep and primal, built into us to ensure our survival, and to help us make course corrections.

Distortions of Fear

If the Natural Emotion of fear is not expressed, it builds up over time – months and years – and can turn into anxiety. A clue about anxiety that can help us to work with it and melt it away is that anxiety is always about the future. We worry about some catastrophe that might happen to us in the next minute, tomorrow, or next year. Thus, to the extent that we can return our attention to the present, the anxiety will diminish. A primary way to be in the present is to say the feeling out loud: "I feel afraid." We can use the five senses to ground ourselves in the present. We can focus on the present moment, what is going on right now. Then anxiety tends to melt away. Another distortion of fear is when we develop a phobia. When the original feeling of fear is not honored and expressed it expands and takes more emotional territory. The fear grows, and then gets locked into place. Ignored, it can go underground and become unconscious. Such fear can be debilitating, especially when it solidifies into forms such as agoraphobia and terror. Entrenched fear holds us prisoner.

A third distortion of fear is panic, which is sharper and more extreme than anxiety. Panic can produce physiological symptoms such as hyperventilation, sweating, and even uncontrolled bodily movements, literally shaking with fear. Panic can make us act in harmful and dangerous ways. When we panic, we lose sight of the purpose of fear, caution and reason; we forget or block out awareness that our actions, including what we say, may have negative consequences. Again, the natural feeling, and its expression, is paramount. We do not always have to go into the explanation of *why* we are afraid, or *what* is making us fearful. Quite often, we cannot control that. But we can feel what we feel, let it be known to ourselves and we can take action to express it.

I Am Not Elisabeth

After several years of attending the Life, Death and Transition workshops designed and taught by Elisabeth Kübler-Ross, the well-known author of the book *On Death and Dying*, I entered her staff-training program. I had family losses of my own to grieve and the training would be helpful in my grief counseling practice and with the Center for Grieving Children. During my training, Elisabeth had appreciated my facilitating skill but said that I was too shy to be a staff member. Over several years, her opinion must have changed because she eventually asked me to join her Center's staff and help with workshops. A couple of years later, I flew to Alaska to staff a workshop, and joined other staff members gathering the day before we were to begin. We had meetings to plan our teaching and facilitating responsibilities. Elisabeth was due to arrive the night before we began on Monday. On Monday morning after breakfast I was told I had a telephone call. It was Elisabeth calling from her office in Virginia. She told me that she could not make it to Alaska and that I should lead the workshop. After we hung up, I could feel my stomach tighten with anxiety, knowing that in a couple of hours I was going to have to stand before the seventy or so people who had just arrived for a workshop with the famous Elisabeth Kübler-Ross and tell them that she was not going to be there, and that instead I would be leading the workshop. I was afraid some people would get up and walk out on the spot. I was fearful of my ability to lead the workshop. The time passed quickly as the staff and I got the meeting room ready with chairs, and brought out the workshop equipment and materials. After lunch the moment came. The participants were ready and there was an expectant silence. I stood up and said, "I'm not Elisabeth." I said it so that I would believe this was really happening, and also to tell the truth, and maybe if it was funny it wouldn't be quite so fearful. No one jumped up and ran for the door: OK, one of my fears was resolved. I went on to explain Elisabeth's absence, and said that she was sending all of us love and healing energy to do the work we came to do. Then I went on to lead the workshop. It went well; participants did their work. I learned that I could lead a workshop. What I learned about myself was that I still didn't quite tell the precise truth standing up there in front of everybody that first day. What I didn't say was the true sentence, "I am afraid." Looking back, saying my truth in that short sentence would have eased my fear. Also, I would have provided a model for truth telling that might have been helpful for participants, and maybe even the staff. But the lesson for me was: tell the truth.

The Hair Ball

At another Alaska workshop years later, on the third day when participants were deeply into expressing their Natural Emotions, a Native Inuit woman came up front to do her work on the mattress. She lamented the many losses her village people suffered from fishing and hunting accidents due to the deadly combination of alcoholism and extreme weather conditions. She told the stories of her husband, her son and her two brothers lost at sea and in the icy mountains. After she told the stories of her losses, she wailed and cried, clutching her stomach. She expressed great fear that more of her villagers and family would be killed fishing at sea or hunting in the wilderness. To all of us listening intently, she expressed her love for her villagers and family, and her overwhelming fear of losing more of them. Though it seemed to me that she still had more feelings to express, she was tired, and it was time to adjourn for lunch. She got up from the mattress, unsteady on her feet. Other participants went off to lunch, but clearly she was not ready to sit down for lunch in the dining hall. She wanted to go outside, so I walked with her out into the snow. She was still trembling with fear. I followed her as she and two friends from her village went around to the back of the big log building, where it was private and quiet. She knelt down in the snow, with her friends supporting her, and began to choke and gag. Then she vomited into the snow. I watched in amazement to see a small, round brown hairball slide out of her mouth down onto the white snow. It was about the size of a golf ball, and looked slimy and dirty. Her friends acted as if this was a normal occurrence, looked at me, and said, "Now she'll be OK." Indeed, the woman looked relieved; her face was more relaxed. I understood that she had literally expelled her fear, or at least part of it. I knew, better than ever before, that when we are unable or unwilling to express our Natural Emotions outside our bodies – to externalize them – they can develop inside our bodies, such as the workshop participant's hairball, or take another form of dis-ease or illness. Unexpressed, fears are likely to fester and even grow larger, more potent and more debilitating. I realized that if we can express our true feelings before they become physical it is easier and takes less toll on our bodies.

Fear can also offer proof that life changes. When we live in our familiar and habitual life, we usually feel comfort. When we feel fear, it tells us that this is new territory. To cast it in that light can dispel fear. But fear suppressed has double power. All the energy we put into pretending we are not afraid when we are drains energy, energy we need to flee or fight. In less severe situations, simply to acknowledge the presence of fear, to let go of pretending to be 'cool' or 'professional' or 'perfect' can drop the level of fear. Then our energy is available to use fear purposefully, not stuck in false protection. Fear, like anger, can be a brittle and fragile eggshell around our inner being. It is supposedly a protection, but it only serves as a delaying tactic, never touching what is underneath. Nothing changes while we are frozen in fear. And our inner self is still untouched, the same old inner self. Maybe this strategy would work if only everything around us would stand still and never change, but of course everything changes all the time. There is meaning to the exhortation, "Go with the flow."

Storm at Sea

Late one summer as the fall season approached, I agreed to help two friends sail a 40' boat south from Marblehead, Massachusetts. Three of us set out and sailed south past Boston Harbor, through the Cape Cod Canal into Buzzards Bay, by Marion, my childhood home. When I saw the low sandy coastline of the waters where I first learned to sail, I felt nostalgic and a lot older than the little boy who had learned to sail in little dinghies, and later begged my cousins to let me crew for them on bigger sailboats. Now we sailed slowly, in calm seas, outside Block Island into the open ocean east of Long Island. We made a long slow turn south, and passed busy New York Harbor off in the distance. Soon we saw dark clouds building in the western sky. As the afternoon wore on, the wind strengthened and the boat began to roll in the increasing seas. The waves became white caps and the wind began to whistle in the rigging. We were out of sight of land and the weather was deteriorating into a storm, and we began to feel helpless and afraid. We knew that few sheltered harbors were available along the New Jersey shore. The boat was sturdy and well equipped and the three of us were experienced sailors, but we were concerned and anxious. We put our worry into action and, with the last of the daylight, prepared to shorten sail. While one steered, two of us went forward and took in the jib; we hauled down the mainsail, and in its place set a small storm trysail. By now, we were unable to see the horizon due to nightfall and the dark clouds, but the boat felt more manageable. Soon the blackness of night surrounded us completely, close and full of breaking waves and noisy wind. We steered by the dim light of the compass. Soon I became seasick, which increased my fear. I didn't want to go down below into the cabin where it was close and smelly, so I hunkered down in a corner of the cockpit. My friends steered and handled the storm sail. The wind rose and eventually we needed to turn on the engine to stay on course. As the boat tossed around in the rough seas, I slid all over the cockpit floor, getting myself up when I had to lean over the side to vomit. The night wore on, we got tired, and we became more anxious. We were afraid we might run out of fuel, lose the use of our engine, and then be at the mercy of the storm. We checked the fuel level in the gas tanks, and reduced engine speed to conserve fuel. We knew we were somewhere off the New Jersey shore near Cape May, but we didn't know exactly where. In the distance we saw lights and, after a half hour of worried speculation, determined that they were the navigation lights from a fleet of fishing boats. Now an added concern was to avoid the boats and their nets. Our fear intensified. We gave the fleet a wide berth, steering way off course for a while. When we were safely beyond the fishing fleet, we returned to our course. But we did not know our exact location. I continued to be seasick, useless as a crewmember. I had confidence in my friends, but I could hear fear and indecision in their voices. I acknowledged to myself that I was really afraid. In my head, I had images of us running aground on the New Jersey beaches. The night seemed endless. True to our gender stereotype, we men didn't say much about our fear, we just concentrated on sailing the boat safely: not a bad thing to do! Eventually, the sky began to lighten and soon we could see beaches way off to our right. My fear melted away as the sun rose. I felt great relief when we identified a buoy, and then saw a stone breakwater marking the entrance to a protected inlet near Cape May. We motored into the channel and finally found a quiet anchorage. Our spirits lifted, we ate some food and, exhausted, crawled into our bunks to sleep. The next day I left the boat to go home. I carried with me the initiation provided by the trip: the fear, the humility of getting seasick, as well as the beauty and magnificence of the ocean, my survival. At the small regional airport it was fitting that the only available flight home was on an airline called Spirit Airlines.

Even though it is uncomfortable to feel fear, it is an energizing emotion. It can be frightening to admit feeling afraid to family and friends – and workshop participants! – and even more so to enemies. But fear has both reason and purpose because it can propel us into awareness and action. Fear wakes us up to danger and gives us the energy needed to avoid harm. If we had not shortened sail and steered around the fishing fleet, we would have further endangered ourselves. Even though to feel fear is uncomfortable, if we can see underneath the discomfort to the real purpose of fear, we can then use it to create a needed and welcomed measure of safety. If I had remained stuck in my fear to the point of phobia, I would have overreacted and might never have set foot on a sailboat again. I am glad that did not happen! I continue to listen to the purposeful voice of fear, knowing it has something important to tell me, whether I am offshore, or on shore.

Spiritual Practice: "A Safe Place"

Sit by yourself and imagine being in a storm with noise and chaos all around. Make your body as small and contracted as you can. Close your eyes tightly. Wrap your arms around yourself, and breathe through your nose minimally and quietly. Take up as small a space as possible. Don't move. Feel yourself contracted and sheltered, wrapped safely in a shell of protection. Relax into the security of being small but alive, as a seed is tiny yet full of potential. Rest. Allow yourself to be safe and secure. When you are ready, expand your breathing, stretch, and slowly come out of your safe place, knowing that you can return when you need to.

Chapter 6

Love: Expansion

Meditation:
Sit in a comfortable place and picture yourself at the end of a challenging day.
Feel yourself welcomed back home in precisely the way you want: that is what meditation offers you.
Every time you sit in silence, like right now, you are welcomed home.

Love could be at the top of the list of natural emotions, before Grief, Anger and Fear. Natural feelings are in no particular order. Each is unique and described here acknowledging the limitation of words. "Love makes the world go 'round'," and the world seems to stop when it is absent. Without love life can be at its blackest. As hard as love is to describe, we know it when we feel it, and we know when we don't feel it. Just as the other feelings exist, come and go, so does love. Love can be unconscious, yet the degree to which we are aware of it, the better we can live its potential, the more love we can give and receive.

Purpose of Love

The purpose of love is to express who we really are, our authentic self, and share it with the suffering world. We can do this in many ways: in solitude and silence. We can think loving thoughts and send them as energy out into the world. We can choose words of love and affirmation to speak out loud. We can take action, consciously take steps to manifest love, to be kind, to help others. All this must begin with loving ourselves, as self-esteem, for we cannot give what we don't have. To allow and experience love around us is another purpose of love, receiving love from family, friends and the world in which we live. Love's two-way street is necessary to provide mutual support, nurturance and growth and development. In family systems, children quickly learn the available sources of love and what they need to say or do in order to be loved. This is clearly a valuable survival skill when we are young. In this way, children learn how to survive in their families of origin, or for that matter in whatever environment they are in. That's the good news: we can learn how to survive. The bad news is that most of us give up some part of ourselves to receive love. That's OK short-term, because we have to survive in the family system; we need to learn the family rules and roles. To develop survival skills is important, even lifesaving. Unless and until we learn how to receive love, we will burn out and fail in our efforts to be healthy partners, parents and caregivers. When we are open to receive love, then we naturally expand and share our love with the suffering world. When I speak of the purposes of love here, I mean unconditional love, that is, a pure love without manipulation. This love is a gift to be given and received without conditions, qualifications or requirements. This does not mean that our loved ones can do anything they want! We can love a person unconditionally yet not approve of their behavior. We love our children, but when one of them picks up a black magic marker and heads for the white wall, we intervene. And yes we continue to love them, if not their behaviors: a crucial difference. "I love you. It's not OK to draw on the wall. Here is some paper," might be appropriate words.

Snowy Woods

As my mother aged into her mid-nineties and became frail, she spent less time in her favorite light-blue chair in the living room, and more and more time in her bedroom. There, her beloved books and family papers surrounded her. Some of the books she had written herself, and we delighted in reading some of her own poetry to her. She would listen carefully, smile at the end, and say in her forgetfulness, "Who wrote that wonderful poem?" We loved to say back to her, "You did!" and watch her face break into a big grin. To get her settled in her room, we moved furniture around, and I came across a painting I had made as a child around age ten. As I discovered poetry, I had been entranced by the image in Robert Frost's poem, *Stopping By Woods on a Snowy Evening*. It was the first poem I learned by heart, and it created a powerful image in my mind. As a boy I would repeat the poem to myself. I found an old piece of cardboard and some black and white paint, and painted the image that came to me from Frost's words. The painting shows a prominent black fence slanted in the foreground with a forest of bare black trees in back, with big white snowflakes drifting down on the scene. When I told my mother that I'd discovered my old painting, which she'd always liked, she asked me to hang it in her room so she could see it from her bed. I did. It was there on the wall when I came to be with her when she was dying. I'd driven to Massachusetts from Maine, and when I went in to see her, I could see in her eyes that she recognized me but she could only mumble an incoherent word of greeting. But then, with great effort, Mum looked directly into my eyes and said the words, "I love you." Later that day after supper, we were concerned that she might be in pain, so we called the hospice nurse. Because it was the weekend, the on-call nurse who came was not the regular nurse but a stranger. I was worried that she would walk in and ask too many questions, disturb Mum and the quiet calm in her room. I answered the doorbell apprehensively. When I opened the door there stood the hospice nurse, diminutive in stature but with steady eyes and a calm but solid presence about her. I was taken aback because she looked just like my mentor, Elisabeth Kübler-Ross, with the same small frame, direct gaze and intense energy. I ushered her inside and told her briefly that we thought Mum was in pain. She listened to me carefully, and then I showed her into Mum's bedroom. The nurse entered and simply looked around. She said nothing. She took in the many shelves of books. Then she noticed and motioned to my old painting of Robert Frost's woods. She smiled in recognition when I told the origin of the painting. I knew she was just the right person to come to attend to Mum in her last hours. I smiled too, but not at the painting. I smiled because I knew that Elisabeth was having a good laugh watching me respond to the hospice nurse who looked just like her.

Mum was quiet after she received more pain medication. Some hours later, I sat beside Mum's bed holding her hand. I was conscious of being in the room where she did so much of her writing. In this final hour we were surrounded and held by the books of her lifetime. I shared her love of words and the writing process, and felt grateful for our many conversations together. When I'd visit, she'd always ask if we could have a "talk", meaning private time to discuss books and writing. Somehow our conversation always got around to love. I sat beside her, now holding her hand; I watched her breathe there in the bed. She looked peaceful, but her breaths came in and out with a soft ragged sound. I sat there and sent her love and peace, love and peace. I knew other family members, my wife, and my son and his wife, were nearby or about to arrive. My mother's hand felt so thin and bony, and her skin was so soft and tender. Then her breathing slowed down, and her out-breath was very long. I waited for her to breathe in. She did, a short breath. Then another long breath out. I waited for the in-breath, and it came. Then another breath came out. Stillness. No movement. No breath in. She was through. Three breaths, just as the Tibetans say. The room was suddenly, newly, still, and so very quiet. I sat holding my mother's hand, still in the stillness with her. We'd had so much time together as her health declined these last months. I was grateful and felt full of my love for her. My eyes brimmed with tears. I looked over at the painting of the snowy woods, and I felt the serenity. I stayed right in the chair where I was, and continued to hold my mother's hand. Eventually my sister came in with my wife, then my son and his wife arrived, all stunned with surprise to see Mum dead there. We gazed not at each other but at Mum, and we cried tears, each in our own way. My son stood behind me with his hands on my shoulders. Just as my mother's heart had stopped beating, our family had stopped, as if by snowy woods, to treasure a sacred final moment of quiet and peaceful love.

Distortions of Love

When we give up too much of ourselves in order to receive love, our authentic self gets lost or distorted. Beyond survival, life can be much more than just getting by. Love is a two-way street, as I remind volunteers and professionals who are committed to giving time, energy and skill to their work. They report this is the hardest challenge: to receive love – unconditional love – without having to do or say anything to 'deserve' or 'earn' it. Among the many distortions of love are love that smothers and love that demands. We can allow ourselves to become smothered by our need for love, to be so needy that we will do anything to be approved of. Then we have lost who we are and what we naturally feel and want. We learn to modify, adjust and distort our own truth. Because children are smart, intuitive and have built-in survival skills, they know how to answer demands from caretakers who say, or imply, "I will love you if..." Children quickly learn to say whatever the caretakers want to hear. Children use their natural intellect to figure out how to respond when parents say or imply with their behavior, "If you love me, you would..." If we do this over time, i.e. past our childhood, we abandon ourselves. We give up satisfying our needs in order to please others. On the surface, it might seem like a working relationship, but when we look closely, we see it is built on a shaky foundation of deception and pretense. It is a lose-lose manipulation. No one can know what we feel but ourselves. We are responsible for meeting our own needs. When we take the time to know what we need and speak our truth, expressed as our true and natural emotions, that courageous act creates a solid foundation for an honest relationship. That foundation begins when we love ourselves, own up to what we feel inside – who we are and what we need – and have the courage to speak it out loud.

'I' Statements

To choose accurate words to speak the truth is a defining creative act. No one knows our history or our present reality – especially what we feel – but ourselves. To express our truth, we must use the first person pronoun 'I'. When I provided family counseling, often a young couple would come in to my office after the honeymoon period had worn off, or because of some crisis. Typically, the two sat down on the couch together, and began to describe their problems by saying, "We," or, speaking about their partner, "You." I would stop them. I would say, "Helen, would you please sit here?" Then I would say, "John, would please sit over there?" I would separate them as far apart physically in my office as possible. Then I would say, "Now, please speak to each other using 'I' statements. Helen, tell John what you are feeling. John, tell Helen what you are feeling." As they followed my instructions to speak for themselves, the fog of co-dependence and enmeshment would begin to clear, and they would experience each other as individual people, each a separate person who had his or her own unique past experiences and natural emotions in the present moment. I encouraged them to look inside themselves first, and not use the other person to find out what they were supposed to feel. When they made the effort, took the time, and had the courage to find and express their own true feeling, it was the beginning of an authentic relationship. Then the miracle can happen: the delicious and affirming experience to say and show who we really are, our spirit, and our essence. Often to our deepest surprise, we can be loved *precisely* for that essence. We don't have to pretend, or scheme, or remember what the other person likes or dislikes about us. We truly can be our unique self and be loved. Really, this is the only way we *can* be loved, for our self, for who we really are. This is the necessary foundation for healthy relationships, to ourselves and to other people.

Eternal Life

Near the end of my studies in California to become an interfaith minister, I felt excited and grateful because I was approaching the completion of more than four years of study and travel. I appreciated all those people, both at home and at my school, who had loved and supported me in my commitment to study ministry. I thought of my supporters as our small class drove together in a van to the rural art studio of a silkscreen artist to make our Ordination stoles. Through the day I worked to choose colors, then drew and painted my silk stole. I thought I was finished, and stood back to admire the colorful stole stretched out in front of me in the sun on the worktable. Suddenly I was filled with gratitude for being able to leave home and come across the country to California to study ministry. I was elated at nearing the milestone of ordination as an interfaith minister. I felt profoundly grateful and graced. I felt suffused in the love of the Divine, held by Creation herself as I gazed down at my new stole, and surprised I had created something so beautiful. Full of this feeling of love, I heard the words 'eternal life' and knew these words belonged on my ordination stole. So I added the final touch to my stole by writing the words 'Eternal Life' on the silk in front of me. Those words became part of my spiritual practice, distilling my existence down to its essence, life everlasting here and now in the spiritual realm. I use them as a mantra, and often remember them when I am providing spiritual care in end-of-life and deep grief settings. I encounter them often in religious and spiritual readings. They remind me of that creative moment in the sun in California when I made my stole, and of the abundant and eternal love of the Universe available to me.

Thursday Morning

Our need for and understanding of love changes over time, because our needs evolve as we grow older and age. This evolution is a natural and healthy process, yet we must have ways of staying current with who we are in the given moment, how we love and are loved. With maturity comes the wisdom to seek help. Counseling, therapy and workshops can offer deeper healing of the distortions of love. In the five-day Kübler-Ross workshops, we encouraged the participants, who either had life-threatening illnesses or were caring for people who did, to express their natural emotions. Their natural love, for themselves and others, had been overshadowed and distorted by life's challenges and tragedies: accidents, disease, disappointments, chronic disease and terminal illness and death. Participants poured out their grief, anger, fear and love. We shared and witnessed deeply moving stories. This emotional sharing and externalization continued for three full days, and into the nights, sometimes until after midnight. On Thursday morning, in Elisabeth's workshop design, the emotional expression was over and the topic was spirituality. I walked into the meeting room to greet the participants. I felt as if I were walking into a spacious cathedral full of love. Even though it was the same room we'd worked in all week, the room now felt enormous, as if it had tall ceilings and stained glass windows to let in the morning sunlight transformed into many colors. I felt a deep sense of wonder and peace, an abundance of acceptance and love. Workshop participants and our staff who had gathered as strangers were now a community. Having shared so much emotion together, participants were full of love, the relief and love of expressing their authentic feelings and having them affirmed and validated.

While this dynamic begins with individual responsibility and awareness, it can also happen with groups of people. The challenge is that no one in our families, in our circle of friends, knows what we are feeling; no one else can determine our unique and specific needs, only ourselves. As adults, we are no longer dependent on others to meet these needs. It is our responsibility. When we love ourselves, it offers us the permission and encouragement to speak and act the way we want and need to. When someone else objects to how we speak, what we say, or how we act, what we do – and it will happen – we need to ensure that we be true to ourselves. Then it is time to take a deep breath and honor our self. What the other person says or does is not our problem. We certainly don't, at this critical point, want to fall back into the trap of changing who we are in order to get the love of the other person, even if they express love for us (see Chapter 8: Living Our Essence). We are capable of loving from the solid place of self, where we appreciate who we are, love our essence, and believe that we are lovable and have love to offer the world. In those meeting rooms on Thursday mornings, love was shining from many faces.

Spiritual Practice: "Flowing Hearts"

Find a peaceful time and place to sit *as you are* – you do not need any special props. Imagine that you are in the presence of wise and loving people, guests from the spiritual realm. These guests are spiritual masters, women and men from the ancient traditions and tribes who come now into your awareness for the sole purpose of loving you. All of them – and there are many – surround you physically and wrap you in their love, a pure and powerful love flowing from their hearts into your heart. Your only task is to receive what is being freely offered. Breathe this abundant love into your heart, let it join with the blood of your heart and be distributed throughout your whole body. This love floods your being, and brings reassurance, abundance, comfort, energy, strength and confidence. And as long as you keep breathing, and remain aware, your spiritual guests continue to bring you all the love you need.

Part II

Practicing Our Essence

Chapter 7

Awareness of Essence

Meditation:
Be like a smooth round stone sitting peacefully grounded in its place on the earth, all its surface open and shining.

Let's use the foundation of Part I as a platform to dive deeper into the practice of living our essence. To do this we need awareness. The crucial quality of awareness is the cornerstone of Gestalt Therapy, which Laura and Fritz Perls taught in the 1960s. I

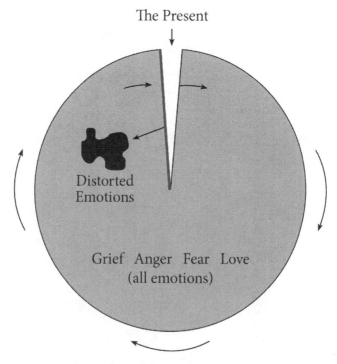

The Present
↓

Distorted
Emotions

Grief Anger Fear Love
(all emotions)

The Gestalt Awareness Cycle

learned Gestalt theory and practice in workshops at Associates for Human Resources in Concord, Massachusetts, in a yearlong graduate program at the Gestalt Institute of Cleveland and with George Cloutier, a Maine psychiatrist and workshop leader.

The Gestalt Awareness Cycle is a circle that represents our unconscious that contains all the natural emotions we have ever experienced. They are hidden in the darkness of time and ignorance. The thin slice out of the top represents the here and now, what we are aware of in the present moment. (I teach this model so much that some students began calling it Jacob's Pie.) This is a model of health; the health is the movement of our natural emotions – one at a time – clockwise around up into the present, into the light of awareness. We are conscious of the emotion in the here and now. When one feeling pops out into the slice at the top that represents the present moment, and is identified, we have the 'Aha' experience: I know what I am feeling now. Though our feelings might come up quickly, one right after another, we have room for only one at time. This is helpful; we can recognize it, identify it, and express it.

According to Gestalt therapy's model of health, when a feeling is not known and expressed, it becomes toxic. When the feeling is known and expressed, the need to know and express it drops away, back into the unconscious. Thereby – and this is the punch line – we create space for the next feeling to come up into awareness and be expressed. Most of this feeling is inside, unconscious, while the expression, the externalization, is outside, conscious, as we put out into the world what was formerly locked away. Because every feeling longs to be felt and expressed, this movement to the slice of openness at the top – the present – is natural, organic and inevitable. In fact, the movement of feelings can define health. That is what feelings seek, every minute and over the years, movement and expression. In fact, feelings are so strong and persistent they *will* be felt and expressed in some form.

If it's not expressed as a natural emotion, a feeling will find its way out as a physical symptom. We now know that unexpressed grief may express as chronic coughing or colds: the fluid of tears showing up inside the body. Unexpressed anger sometimes manifests as heart disease. An unrecognized need for love may come as a series of unhealthy love affairs. Writers like Louise Hay, Caroline Myss and Joan Borysenko detail these possibilities.

The Tapping on My Shoulder

For me, an unrecognized, unexpressed feeling is like a persistent hand tapping on my shoulder. If I don't give the feeling what it wants, acknowledgement and expression, the tapping gets more insistent. The feeling pulls more and more of my attention away from the present moment. If I ignore this feeling, over time it robs me of my ability to function in the present. The unexpressed feeling eventually will become raucous and demanding, and insist that I pay attention. The tapping on my shoulder says, "Hey, remember me, I'm your sadness about how your father treated you." That's what the sadness, or any emotion, wants: attention, acknowledgement, and expression, conscious expression. Conscious means, "I know this is sadness." If I don't say to the sadness, "OK, I hear you, you're right. I do feel sad about that," the sadness will pounce on every natural loss I feel, in this case about men and authority, and grow larger and more insistent. Eventually it will become a 2" x 4" club whacking me on my head emotionally until I do pay attention. Some people think they can simply 'channel' their anger into physical activity such as sports or exercise. But for healing to occur, consciousness is required. We must be conscious that we have the feeling. We may or may not know its cause – that part is optional. Consciousness and externalization are not optional.

There are times when the present situation or the people around me do not feel safe enough for me to be vulnerable and share my intimate emotions. In this case, it is healthy *not* to express my feelings. I must acknowledge that I *feel* them, at least to myself, but then I can put them on a metaphorical shelf. I promise them I will get back to them soon, within days. Then when it is safe, I can invite them into my present awareness and give them what they seek: expression. We can plan a Shelf Day when we create the time, space and energy to reach up to our 'shelf' and invite whatever feelings we've put there to come down so that we can express them. A benefit of doing this is to remind our self that we have control over whether, when, how, and to whom we express our feelings. It is a great gift to our self to acknowledge and express a long-suppressed emotion. First this act frees up energy, and second, it keeps the awareness moving, and as we've seen, this movement is a key to health.

Often the most challenging and the darkest times are when we feel 'stuck'. What is stuck is this movement into awareness and the subsequent expression of emotion. When we have the courage to express the truth of what we feel, that slice of present awareness at the top of the circle opens to receive the next feeling; we can be responsive to whatever comes next. We are back in the flow of our lives, our energy no longer drained or blocked by a piece of 'unfinished business'. Instead of using up energy to hold back our natural emotions, all our energy is available in the present, to express our authentic emotions, who we really are, our essence.

Another quality of health is the recognition that the *process* of awareness and movement is more important than the *content* of what we are aware of. The expression is more important than what we express. This goes against the messages from our reduc-tionist, ego-based culture, which wants to know not only *what* the feeling is but also *why* we feel it. The culture wants a rationale for the story, a justification. To try to satisfy the culture's obsession with exactly what the feeling is, and why we feel it, propels us quickly up into our heads. Our mind wants to fix the 'problem', to find a solution. Our intellect tries to figure it out.

And if we can't come up with exactly what the feeling is or a valid reason why we feel it, suddenly we have lost permission to feel it. But it is our responsibility to give ourselves the permission to do what we need to do to be healthy – feel our natural emotions that are tapping on our shoulder. Sometimes that means trusting the validity of the feeling without knowing where it came from. That is the beauty and power, even the purity, of a natural emotion. To honor the feeling, to be healthy, we give it expression.

My Anger

When my two-year-old son's mother and I were breaking up, and she decided to take him out of state to live, I was sad and angry. My friends, sympathetic, understood my sadness but focused on what I could do to stay in touch with my son. But I was full of anger and needed to express it. I couldn't make definite plans to see my son unless and until I expressed my anger. This dilemma got me to my first workshop with Kübler-Ross. On the second day of the workshop I watched other participants walk to the front of the room to tell their stories and vent their emotions, but I couldn't see myself being that vulnerable. An hour later I found myself on the mattress with Elisabeth sitting beside me. Elisabeth encouraged me to express my natural anger and fear about losing touch with my little son. I yelled and raged at my son's mother. I could feel something changing. Then Elisabeth said to me, "You're sad and angry about losing your son, but you are also sad and angry about the little two-year-old boy you have inside you who was taught to suppress his natural emotions." More tears and rage burst out of me. I cried and I yelled. Soon memories from events early in my life came to me. I learned that once I could express my sadness and anger about my present life, I could follow the emotional thread back to express the old feelings, too. The cleaning and clearing that resulted allowed me to live more fully in the present, awake and aware of my feelings as they came up. It was healing, though I felt vulnerable doing it, to tell the story of my son, and my own little boy inside me. Though there are times to tell our stories, i.e. how we came to feel a particular emotion, the expression of the feeling itself is much more important. This is because of the deep and restorative truth that we are not our story, and no matter our story, we are not our *feeling* about the story. We are individuals feeling a feeling, and as we become aware of it, we can consciously move the feeling out of our unconscious, bring it around the circle, and up into the sliver of present awareness. Then we can grant its wish to be expressed. Once I expressed my anger at my son's mother, I could feel my love for him, and even some compassion for his mother. Reconnected to my love for my son, I felt enormous relief. I experienced a new compassion – even tenderness – for my own deep emotional life, and for that which lies underneath my natural emotions. At the workshop, I had the opportunity to express my changing feelings, grief, anger, sadness, love, and I also had a glimpse into what doesn't change, my spirit.

Toxic Pool

When we decide for whatever reason – and good reasons exist short-term – that we don't want to express the feeling, we can let it move back into unconsciousness, and there it sits, quiet for the moment. But if it is not expressed, over time, the feeling builds up. The unexpressed feeling grows and becomes a toxic pool, and sits there off to one side, where it festers and drains energy from the present. Then two things can happen. One, this 'pus pocket' of unexpressed emotion can leak into the present moment, spreading its poison. For example, if the repressed feeling is anger, then we are grumpy a lot of the time. We notice and reflect back the negativity of the world. If the repressed feeling is sadness, then we are melancholy; sometimes our faces have a little tear line running down our face under our eyes. We are overly sensitive to the sadness around us. If the repressed feeling is fear, we might live with a low level of anxiety. We become fearful, afraid of life. We reflect back the fear rampant in the world. If we are feeling but not expressing love, then we might experience a series of short-term unfulfilling relationships. We might remain in a relationship too long, trying to make it work. We reflect back the distortions of love around us. We feel the absence of love.

Two, the toxic pool of unexpressed emotion can burst into the present. This might be explosive and even lethal as when natural anger turns to rage. Remember, the health of this model is in the movement. We can become aware of what we feel and we can express the feeling in the moment. The extraordinary and lifesaving gift of living this model is that the present, that slice out of the top, keeps coming around again, over and over, moment to moment. This I find very hopeful. The recurring present offers us countless new opportunities for awareness, and thus new opportunities to uncover our feelings and express what we need to express. It's even easier than that: our feelings have a fierce energy that seeks to be released. So it's a question of us joining a flow already in process. The flow of our feelings moving around the circle and up to awareness is their natural motion. It's what they long to do. The longing and persistence of our feelings to express themselves gives us a profoundly healthy quality with which to live our lives.

Whales after the Workshop

My friend and colleague, George Cloutier, a psychiatrist and pilot, brought his Augusta Mental Health Institute patients out to Great Duck Island, 12 miles into the ocean off Acadia National Park, to give them opportunities for group therapy and community living in primitive conditions. Gestalt therapy groups met every evening, and Gestalt weekend workshops were open to the public. George and I co-led an intense weekend workshop during which participants unleashed stories of suffering and tragedy, and all the attendant natural emotions, especially anger and sadness. Afterwards, late Sunday afternoon, George and I took a walk through the woods to the airstrip to debrief and to share what we'd experienced and learned at the workshop. Then we climbed into George's old seaplane. He revved the engine and we bumped along the rocky airstrip set in the middle of the island. We took off and flew around the island, looking down at the geodesic dome and scattered cabins, and then headed east. We were looking for whales that sometimes swam by Mount Desert Rock. We flew through the hazy sky with the wide ocean below, and I felt my heart expand from the successful workshop, the expression of so much anger, sadness and love, the work we'd all done to help participants release old distorted feelings. I felt the openness of sky above and sea below. We'd left behind the hard work of facilitating the workshop, witnessing all the natural emotions, and entered a new spaciousness and beauty. We flew farther east into a light haze from the smoky southwest wind. Then in the late afternoon sun, we came to Mount Desert Rock, where the sea shimmered around the lighthouse, surrounded by rocks and breaking white waves. We circled several times, then saw whales below: large, long, low black forms swimming slowly underneath us, flowing through the sea. They seemed still, but swam slowly, majestically, leaving white wakes of water that widened behind them in the green sea. My senses were newly alive and I could drink in the beautiful powerful creatures below me. They seemed free and magnificent, just as we humans feel when we express what is inside us.

Awareness of life as beauty in the moment is a clearing and cleaning process. As we become more and more aware, invite more and more feelings into expression, the pathway to expression becomes scoured, cleansed, and more open. This process is self-supporting because it reinforces the health of the flow of feeling. A lightness develops, a confidence that we do not have to be stuck, that we can let a feeling come up into awareness, and not have to know everything about it, where it came from, or when it happened. This is a process that demands trust. We must trust that we have a right to feel the emotion even without knowing its source. Why? Simply because we feel it, that's all. It's enough that we feel it. For the moment we feel it. Someday we will not feel it. Feelings come and go. The stunning realization comes that it does not matter what the feeling is, which one of the many feelings of being human. It matters only that we become aware of the feeling, keep it flowing and express it safely. We are not what we feel, but our feelings point the way to who we are, our essence. While our feelings are the beginning expressions of our spirit, it is our spirit that is the one constant foundation underneath all of this movement, this constant feeling and expression of emotion. Our feelings originate from and express our larger spirit, our essence, who we are at the most fundamental level.

Spiritual Practice: "I Am Aware"

As you sit quietly, visualize a big circle with a slice out of the top. In the body of the circle, see your unconscious that contains your natural emotions. See the thin slice of awareness at the very top of the circle, shining with light and openness, ready, available, that invites your next awareness and expression. Now imagine an endless flow of your emotions – one at a time – moving around, up into that slice, having their time in the sun. Then, acknowledged and expressed, they drop away down into the soup of unconsciousness, thereby creating space for the expression of another essence, over and over again, without end, a stream of countless expressions of authentic feeling. Rejoice in the flow!

Chapter 8

Living Our Essence

Meditation:
I watch myself breathing in and out.
Now I watch the one who watches.

While awareness of our feelings is crucial, we must continue to move from theory to practice, from imagining to living, from the head to the heart. This progression is thwarted by the continuation of old behavior patterns we adopted in our childhood. Though these patterns can be positive and even creative strategies to survive in our childhood family systems, if unexamined and continued into adulthood, they seriously impede and distort our ability to lead fulfilling lives of essence. The concept of the Victim Triangle is central to learn how to express natural emotions and live our essence. Early in our lives, in an attempt to escape pain, we play one or more of the three roles described by the Victim Triangle model. We subvert our true self to gain approval from our family. We create a false self; we pretend to be someone we aren't. It is a crucial part of our healing to identify these Victim Triangle roles. The spiritual journey leads through the discovery of our natural emotions, their acknowledgement and expression, and thus out of the role-playing described by the Victim Triangle. As we walk this path, suffering burns away the ego to illuminate the authentic self, our essence.

The Victim Triangle Model

The model of the Victim Triangle originated with the Transactional Analysis work of Eric Berne, which showed the interactions and communications between people. It describes in

The Victim Triangle

Perpetrator/Persecutor

Rescuer/Caretaker

Ways Out

1 – Find natural child's needs and feelings and express them

2 – Say "No, thank you."

3 – Do it without excuses.

4 – Refuse the payoff

Victim

diagram form the roles people may adopt to try to avoid pain as they relate to each other. It is a model of ill-health, a diagram of a human being attempting to get his or her needs met by choosing a coping role, a role they no doubt have seen demonstrated in their family of origin. To play a role, while it seems easier in the moment, prevents heart-centered authentic speech and action and distracts us from living an authentic life. This role-playing is unconscious, unaware behavior. In the stress of the moment, to try to survive, to avoid suffering, we forego our natural feelings, subvert or ignore our essential being, our authentic self, and adopt a role that we believe will get us through the crisis unscathed. In addition, in a continuous attempt to avoid suffering, we assign a corresponding role to other people. So we play the game of living out roles for each other, reverting to unconscious behavior, all in the name of survival.

The problem is that we continue to play the role long after the early need for it has lapsed. We trap ourselves in the role; we get stuck in pretense, and even in performance: it worked once, why can't it work again? But no relationship can be healthy when both individuals pretend to be someone they aren't and play a role instead of being authentic. We develop the ability to leave the Victim Triangle only when we accept that we did experience suffering, and become aware of the natural emotions of our experiences and express those feelings.

We know we are caught in the Victim Triangle when:

We don't know what we're feeling.
We know what we're feeling but can't or won't express it.
We feel 'stuck' and not seen as our self.
The words we speak don't feel or sound like ours.

It feels like both people are losing: it's a lose-lose interaction.

There is a false positive payoff for the transient experience of 'better or 'worse than'. Note that this is still a comparison, where the attention remains on the other person, and not our own self.

We play any of the three roles of the Victim Triangle – and sometimes all of them – to attempt to escape pain. The roles we adopt are the Victim, the Judge/Perpetrator and the Caretaker/Rescuer.

Early in our lives, or yesterday morning, our ego, thinking it's oh-so-clever, reprises a familiar role in order to avoid pain and suffering. It seems to work for a while. How we've been acting, what we've been doing, has become locked into place, has become our role. We think it is an easier path, so we grab a pre-written, dog-eared script, crafted for us by family members and our culture. We even adopt the role's physical posture, and automatically read the script's lines. No, the words don't sound like ours, because they aren't, but they're handy, familiar, and seem to take care of the immediate need to say and/or to do something that avoids embarrassment, discomfort or pain. The role offers us an easy identity and course of action, something quick to say or do. When integrity and wholeness are abandoned like this, co-dependence is born. Welcome to the Victim Triangle.

The triangle is the strongest geometric figure, and will stay intact if everyone continues to play his or her rigid roles. However, the minute one person makes a change the system begins to fail. Each person playing a role depends on the others playing theirs. The Victim Triangle is a dependent system: people playing their roles depend on other people playing theirs. It is a dependency-producing system that enmeshes its players in cartoon-like lives that are barren, devoid of authentic feelings. Another problem when we play these roles is that the longer we play them, the more out of touch with our feelings we become. I remember people looking up at me from the workshop mattress they were pounding in frustration, saying, "I don't know who I am anymore!"

The Victim Role

As newborn children, we are helpless and dependent on others for our life and our care, and in that sense we begin life as Victims. This is the first role we adopt. Then when we first have the experience of not getting our needs met, we blame our parents, but that is not safe because they are the ones who gave us life, and they probably are meeting at least some of our needs. So we blame ourselves. This is the beginning of living in the Victim Triangle as a victim with low self-esteem and shame. Another name for the Victim Triangle is the "No or Low Self-Esteem Triangle". In further attempts to survive, we scheme and manipulate: How can I satisfy my need for attention and love? How can I avoid Dad yelling at me? How can I get Mom to stop hitting me? What do I need to do to stop my uncle from touching me in a way that feels disgusting? If playing the victim doesn't work, we find another role that does. A victim tries to get his or her survival needs met by attracting protection and care, and then blaming others for being a victim when that desired protection and care is not forthcoming. Ironically and paradoxically, a person playing a victim often wields a lot of power. But it is 'power over', not healthy empowerment. We know we're relating to a victim when we feel helpless, blamed, and powerless.

The Perpetrator/Judge Role

The Perpetrator/Judge tries to get his or her needs met by criticizing and judging others. We find fault with their actions. To play this role is to avoid responsibility. We try to avoid criticism by criticizing others. Instead of accepting the consequences of our actions, we righteously inform people of what they are doing wrong. We can see this in the 'pecking order' phenomena when a person who has been judged finds a person to judge and becomes a perpetrator. It seems easier to tell other people what's wrong with them than to accept and change what is wrong with us. A person in the Perpetrator/Judge role creates suffering in other people in order to avoid their own suffering. They give people opinions and information instead of listening to their natural emotions. They collect reasons and resources to prove that their judgments are correct. Perpetrators and judges will go to great lengths to prove they are right and should be obeyed. We know we're relating to a Perpetrator/Judge when we feel attacked, or unjustly criticized.

The Caretaker/Rescuer Role

The Caretaker or Rescuer tries to get his or her needs met by finding, even creating, people to take care of and to save. This can be a seductive role to play to avoid feeling pain. When we find a victim to take care of so that we don't have to experience what is wrong and uncomfortable with our own life, we can even enjoy the social benefit to feel righteous and worthy. Our friends and family, and the society around us, will often respond with praise and affirmation if we help people. Expert caretakers create needy victims to care for. The role of care*taker* in the Victim Triangle is that of a thief, someone who *takes* something, responsibility, away from the victim in order to meet his or her own needs. On the other hand, a care*giver* is not stuck in the Triangle. A caregiver offers help without requiring anything in return; their time, energy and skill are a true gift, freely and lovingly offered without any compensation needed. A care*taker* is a thief, taking something of value away from a person. What they are taking is responsibility, dignity and respect. We know we're relating to a caretaker when we feel smothered by attention and told what to do.

Sailors at the Door

During the Second World War, when I was two years old, my father was serving in the United States Navy, aboard escort ships protecting convoys of tankers and freighters sailing to England. In our New York City apartment, my mother and I lived with the fear of Dad's ship being torpedoed and sunk, and of him never coming home again. One evening the doorbell rang and when Mum, with me by her side, opened the door, we saw two uniformed sailors standing in the hall. My mother, thinking they had come to deliver bad news, fainted briefly. I got down on the floor and hugged her and tried to comfort her. Right then I assumed the role of caretaker. The sailors quickly assured us that they were there only as a courtesy, to say hello, and see if we needed anything. Still, we were relieved when they left. As a scared little boy, I had found a role to avoid my own feelings of fear of my dad's death by taking care of my mother's fear. I learned that when I took care of another person's fear by becoming a caretaker, I could avoid my fear, at least for the moment. A pattern began, a pattern that found other uses as our family grew. Soon I had two younger sisters, and after that a new brother. Being resourceful, as kids are, when I wanted to avoid my own feelings, I quickly found ways to take care of my siblings.

Leaving the Victim Triangle

To leave the Victim Triangle means to learn how to acknowledge and express natural emotions and, therefore, to live authentically. First, we must accept that we did experience suffering. Then we allow ourselves to become aware of the emotions produced naturally by our experiences of suffering, and express those feelings. The way out of the Victim Triangle is awareness, which was highlighted in the previous chapter. When we can witness our responses, observe how we speak and interact, we can choose to move beyond the roles of Victim, Perpetrator/ Judge and Caretaker/Rescuer. The path out of the Victim Triangle is to change the transactions *between* roles in the corners of the triangular model. It is the interactions between roles that we can change, shifting the language and behavior, the communications and actions. The interactions are the weakest parts of the triangle, and thus the easiest to change. We will not have success if we try to exit the triangle through the corners, the strongest and sharpest places, where our family and friends are probably entrenched as they play out their roles. They likely will not respond to our attempts to confront and change them. In fact they are likely to get quite defensive; they *like* their roles, and are not about to give them up without a fight. We do not have control over what another person says or does, but do have control over how we respond and what we say. We can change the way *we* relate to other people by choosing different words and actions, expressing our true natural emotions and speaking as and for our authentic essential self. Our healing from playing roles is not dependent on anyone else but ourselves. These five tasks assist us out of the triangle:

Find the natural child's needs and feelings and express them.
Say "No." If you're polite, it's "No, thank you."
Say or do it without excuses, or without having to have a reason.

Refuse the payoff, the manipulation, the 'deal'.
Refuse playing the 'false self'.

To express feelings requires safety, i.e. a safe time, a safe place and a safe (non-judgmental) person so that we can trust and use the information being generated by our five senses: sight, touch, hearing, smell and taste, plus that all-important sixth sense, intuition. Remember that the path out of the Victim Triangle is not a four-lane, one-way Interstate Highway with illuminated road signs and convenient fuel and rest stops, leading straight to the promised land of authenticity and freedom! No, at first it is a mere track in the woods – the road not taken – overgrown with prickly vines and seductive with false turns. But precisely because it is hard to find, we know it is not someone else's path, but our own. Mary Oliver's powerful poem, *The Journey*, describes this passage with great hope, for the traveler moves over the debris of his/her life striding deeper into the world, overcoming fear to lead his/her own unique life.

We are creating our path anew, uniquely ours. When we exercise our courage and begin the walk, or crawl, out of the Victim Triangle, it is slow going, as we work our way past obstacles and other people's objections and protestations. But every step is reinforced by a sense of rightness, of being who we really are. We find a built-in confirmation and strength as we forge ahead on our path. And as we continue on this path away from playing roles, we can find fellow travelers such as friends, colleagues, participants in a group, or, especially precious, a person within our own family. We can create comforting companionship on our walk to freedom. Eventually, as we experience a new freedom outside the triangle, we will look back at the old system behind us and breathe a sigh of relief, or give a shout of ecstasy.

Out of the triangle for the first time, we suddenly look around and realize we are all alone. It may feel like we are lost on a brand new planet, and we are not even sure the air is safe to breathe. We do not have a compass or a map to show the way. We can feel alien in this new territory. But then, when we summon the courage to take a breath, stay a while in this new place, feel the firm ground underneath our feet, keep our eyes open, take another breath of fresh air, and inhabit our new space, a miracle happens: we look around and see another person who is nearby. He or she is speaking and acting from his or her own truth. They want us to be authentic, too. And then another person shows up, and another. We are not alone. We have people around us, people who are making their own journey out of their personal triangles. In fact, as we become more and more our true self and able to share our essence, we literally will attract people to us, people who appreciate honesty and authenticity. Seeing us, they see a healthy person; they take heart, and gain permission to be true to themselves by leaving the Victim Triangle behind.

Getting Sucked Back In

Eventually, inevitably, a crisis develops in our families. An important family event or anniversary comes along, a special wedding or graduation, perhaps a birth or a death. A sibling gets envious of our newfound freedom, or the holiday season arrives with our family's expectations and traditions. Or this happens in our current life, in our work, in organizations, agencies or businesses where the Victim Triangle roles get reconstituted. Suddenly we feel a strong pull backwards, as if a magnet were dragging us back into the Triangle. The family or work crisis reignites our old role, and we begin to speak that role's language and take that role's actions. There are people back there in the triangle that we love, and who love us. They are saying, "Don't leave! Come back! Be your old self! Be the person we recognize!" "Be the person who supports me in playing my role." At this point, we have a choice. We can choose to go back into our old role, our false self, but with our new awareness, and for a limited time. We can decide to show up for a family event, but we don't have to stay. We can remind ourselves that when we are stuck in the Victim Triangle roles, we are stuck playing our false self, stuck in suffering. Indeed, the Buddhist word for suffering can be translated as 'stuck' (see Chapter 7: Awareness of Essence). When we're stuck back in our old role, and the old seductive voices are making us comfortable, we can be conscious that we have choices; we can choose new language, a language of authenticity. A key word useful when we get sucked back in old Victim Triangle roles is, "No." We can say it to others; we can say it to our self. No is a complete sentence. Of course, if we were brought up in a family where manners were valued, like me, we can add, "No, thank you." But the point is to say, "No". We can say "no" to an outdated role and therefore say "yes" to our authentic self. Saying "no" sometimes means we say to family members, "No, that's not what I feel." "No, I'm not going to do that anymore." We can say, "This is what I feel." "This is what I am going to do." We can be more conscious that we have choices about how we behave. Simply to remember that we have choices is itself empowering and transformational, and can facilitate leaving the triangle instead of getting sucked back into the old roles.

Down From the Pine Trees

When I was married with a family, my wife and I packed up the kids and drove down to visit my parents for the Thanksgiving holidays. After the three-hour drive, we finally turned into their driveway. Amid all the kids' excitement, suddenly, from the pine trees above, the Victim Triangle pounced down on me. The old script was dog-eared but I knew it well. I went into my parents' house with the script in mind, walked over to my mother and said, "How are you feeling, Mum? Are you OK?" The Caretaker watched from a corner, smiling approval. But with my newfound awareness of the Victim Triangle, and of the hazards of my habitual role as Caretaker, I listened briefly to my mother, felt honest compassion, and then stepped back. Then I recovered my authentic self and shared news about me and my kids, my truth, and what was going on in my life, especially how I was feeling about it. I had moved from a caretaker to a caregiver. In time, I would tell my siblings, and even my mother, the role I had been playing for many years. I told them how free and relieved I felt to have the new awareness of my old role, and how good I felt to leave it behind and be more authentic.

Staying Out

Sinead O'Connor states this powerfully in her song, "What Doesn't Belong to Me". She describes a key skill in leaving the Victim Triangle: to let go of the responsibility for another person's feelings. It is true that our efforts to leave may produce challenging feelings from friends and family. Some will not approve of our new actions and words. They may even not want to continue the relationship with us. They themselves may plunge deeper and more firmly and stridently into their old roles. Remember the goal here is not to feel good, or to make other people feel good, but to honor our own truth and authenticity.

The foundation for living an authentic life, of being who we are, without apology or explanation, is to speak and act our truth in the present moment. This means we shed these out-of-date roles, both voluntary and involuntary. Our awareness of the limits of these roles – and the cost to play them – brings us to what is underneath awareness: presence and essence. If suffering is identification with roles, then conscious suffering, aware suffering, offers us transcendence, a way to return to authenticity. Here, outside the Victim Triangle where we are truly ourselves, we can be authentic. Here we are at peace with the present situation because we are at peace with who we are in the present. Then we seek others who live authentically, who are not afraid to show and live their essence. This is the foundation for healthy effective and lasting relationships, relationships of essence to essence.

Spiritual Practice: "I Am"

Reflect for a minute which Victim Triangle role is most familiar to you. See yourself caught in that role, and offer yourself appreciation that you had the creativity to find a role that allowed you to survive in your family. Offer yourself compassion for being a survivor. Now recognize the passage of time and your current age and awareness. Know that you can be free of an old role that no longer serves you, and that now you can express and live your truth. You can express your true spirit – who you really are. And you can do this without the need for justification, excuse or rationalization. You are who you are. Say the words, "I am," several times. I am.

Chapter 9

Essence Spiritual Practice

Meditation:
Oh Holy One, please sit here with me, breathe life into me and I will breathe life back into you.

When we leave the roles of the Victim Triangle more and more behind us, and thus live more authentic lives, we can better create our path into the spiritual realm. As natural and human as they are, emotions and the roles we play come and go. Underneath, more constant, is our spirit. Once we begin to be aware of our self as spiritual in nature, suddenly and mysteriously everything we do, everything we are, has the potential to be recognized as it is, spiritual. With this awareness, from this new viewpoint, spiritual practice can be anything and everything we do and are. Our life can be from Spirit, energized by Spirit and in the service of Spirit. We bring Spirit to everything. Spirit brings everything to us. There is no separation, or there doesn't have to be; we can move toward union. We realize everyone is Spirit; everything in the Universe is Spirit, is essence. Miraculously, we realize what has always been true. We wake up to a new reality, as Eckhart Tolle says in his book *A New Earth*: we remember how it has always been, and always will be.

After the hard work described in Part One, the work to identify, feel and express our Natural Emotions, then forge our own path out of the Victim Triangle, the reward is the flowering of our spiritual life. We become aware in a new way, as spiritual beings, more authentically alive, and we experience ourselves as part of the wondrous creative Universe. We want to actively participate in this, our new world, our new earth, our new heaven. Spirit is with us always; we are Spirit no matter what. To develop and maintain new avenues into the spiritual realm, it is useful to know more about our natural spiritual tendencies, and, significantly, ways that the spiritual is already part of our lives. It is comforting to remember that as we reach out to the Divine, the Divine reaches out to us. In order to create and maintain spiritual practices, such as meditation, prayer and art, it is helpful to be conscious of our present spiritual beliefs, for they create and sustain our practices. And they are the foundation for creating new spiritual practices in the future.

Spiritual Beliefs

How we access our beliefs depends on our awareness of how they are already present. We forget sometimes, until we are stunned by a magnificent sunset, or melted by a baby's giggle. Suddenly the belief is so present and easy to recognize. Our beliefs often are quiet, in the background, so that we need to evoke them with our senses and intuition. Sometimes our beliefs must be intentionally activated. This can be like turning on a switch. A firm step must be taken; we must do something definite. Maybe we have the belief, but it's dormant, asleep. In this case, we have to wake it up, accelerate it, and give it energy. This takes intention and intensity. Perhaps a belief needs to be provoked or stimulated. When we know what we don't believe we can illuminate what we do believe. When we investigate unfamiliar religious practices we can appreciate familiar ones. Some beliefs are coy, shy, and ask to be seduced out into our awareness. We remember the pleasure of feeling loved by the Divine as a spiritual belief. Often the task is to uncover a belief that has been forgotten; it's there, but we've been distracted and forgetful. We need to tear away the coverings and open it up. Belief systems are waiting to be discovered; we are called to be explorers. We search out new belief systems as ancient sailors sought out new territories. Spiritual seekers ask questions to find their beliefs. They become spiritual finders. Some key questions are, "When do we pray, meditate or ask to be guided?" Since Spirit is without space or time, it is always available; there is no place where it is not. "What do we believe in?" Believing requires energy. We benefit from putting our belief into words, even if it is only a simple statement. It is a commitment, first to ourselves, then to family, friends and colleagues. Yet, we must remember and have the humility to know that our belief systems change. Life happens, our birthdays accumulate, mysteries deepen, illumination occurs. Our beliefs evolve organically. "What do we hope and dream for?" To bring our hopes and dreams to consciousness is a tender and intimate awakening. Suddenly we are vulnerable and fragile, exposed. Equally, our fears show our beliefs. When we become afraid of abandonment and suffering, what or who we turn to shows what we believe in. In the face of adversity, we want to confirm that God, the Divine, cares about us. "Which emotion encourages our spirit to emerge?" From earlier chapters we know that to access and to express our feelings shows us what we believe. Specific emotions trigger corresponding beliefs, and together provide a wealth of resources. Our belief systems guide us forward toward essence. Other questions designed to awaken spiritual belief systems are listed in the Afterword section in the back of the book.

My Practice

Spiritual practice is the way to put our spiritual belief systems into action, to give them a place in our lives. Spiritual practice is both the conscious intention and the planned consistent action to bring the spiritual into the forefront of our lives; it is woven into the everyday fabric of our lives. In this way, we create our lives as an integral part of the unseen yet all-powerful spiritual realm; we have a place in the greater Universe, a home in communion with all of creation. I find it useful to bring spiritual practice to the beginning of my day, in the early morning. It is quiet in my house then. I am still close to the unconscious state of sleep when my mind was resting, so it is uncluttered. Going right from my bed to my meditation cushion works well for me. I like to have an established morning ritual: I can slide into it without needing to think. A large wooden Buddha sits on my altar waiting for me. Buddha's calm energy welcomes me into the room and into my practice. To create the space and time for spiritual practice is a statement to myself that this is so important that it comes first. Everything else in my day can flow from that sacred beginning. Spiritual practice – anytime – is the way to practice being who I truly am. To practice means to engage in regularly, to create a daily pattern of behavior, to act, to use energy with intention. Just like practicing to play the piano, or play tennis, regular spiritual practice builds skill and offers continual reassurance of our home in the spiritual realm.

Encouragement for spiritual practice comes from many sources. Sometimes we are inspired (in-spirited) towards spiritual practice by a teacher or scriptural writing, or when we encounter a powerful nugget of wisdom from an everyday happenstance. Sometimes a personal crisis brings us to our knees, appropriately the attitude of prayer. In our vulnerable state, after all else fails us, after we've expressed our natural emotions and worked through and left the roles of the Victim Triangle, what we have left is the spiritual. We may find a fragile hope that something exists beyond this present despair that will hold us like a tender and reassuring parent. The hope might appear like a gentle lover, who whispers endearments that offer tiny candle-lights of hope in the dark night of the soul, presaging the dawn. It is then, in the quiet of dawn, that I find the inner peace and the outer peace to begin again. No matter the nighttime dreams just past or the daytime tasks that beckon, here is a sweet possibility, a few present moments of time and space. This is the opportunity to enter that spiritual realm where there is no time, where there is no space, and be. The only thing I can do is 'be', be there, be here, and be present. The word practice is accurate, because practice means to keep at it. It is not a failure when a thought appears. It is not a relapse when a sound disturbs me. I know my mind, and distractions are inevitable. It's what the mind does. Thank you. Back to meditation. Return. Return again. Watch my breath. Say my mantra. Experience my abdomen rising and falling. Again. Notice my breath coming in and going out. Whatever it takes. Whatever brings me back to who I am, sitting there. Breathing in, breathing out. Practicing. The Buddhists remind us to practice for the day of our death. We breathe in, we breathe out, preparing for that moment to come when we breathe out, and do not breathe in.

Office Fire

The path to spiritual practice can appear unexpectedly. In fact, a reliable sign of spiritual authenticity is mystery. Years ago, my grief counseling home office mysteriously caught fire. I was upstairs and smelled smoke. I rushed downstairs into my office and found a wall in flames. I closed the door, got my wife and our children, who had just come home from school, out of the house, and called the fire department. I sat in despair on the curb across the street, waiting for the fire trucks to arrive. I watched smoke pour out of my office windows. I was consumed with feelings: love for my family and relief and gratitude that none of them had been injured, grief over my books, papers, furniture, and gifts from clients and workshop participants burning, anger at the unknown cause of the fire. I was anxious and fearful about what the extent of the damage would be, and how I would pay for the repairs. Though I didn't know it then, sitting there on the curb, I was in a state of shock and prayer. This was a crisis that brought me to my knees, there on the curb, a crisis that challenged and changed my conception of my professional counselor self, and my self as a father and husband. If anyone had seen me there on the sidewalk and said something like, "There, there, Jacob, this will turn out to be a good thing, a positive event in your life," I would have slugged them. I needed to feel all my natural emotions. I needed to feel them, express them and find out what was underneath them, who I was feeling all those feelings. For me, it was purification by fire. My tears burned away old patterns and beliefs about myself, as eventually I began to find a deeper sense of purpose about my life and work. When I recovered from the shock of the fire, I felt and expressed my anger, grief, sadness, fear and love to my family and friends. As the chaos and disruption receded behind me, I found a new clarity. I felt the tender and fierce love for my children and my wife, and the grace of my work in the emotional and spiritual realms. The expression of these natural emotions had scoured out a path to my soul – bared my soul. I knew I wanted to live close to my soul – my essence – and the counseling profession felt old to me, outdated. I was overwhelmed by the multitude of stories my clients were telling me, all that drama. I wanted to live in the realm of spirit, and to provide spiritual care – care giving – as my work in the world. I walked slowly and painfully, along the path out of the Victim Triangle, and left behind the familiar but outworn role of grief counselor, of caretaker, into the new territory of living and working as a spiritual caregiver. Years later, I can say yes, the fire in my office was a positive, transformative event. It helped me hear a still, small voice inside whispering to me that counseling was no longer my profession. I now understood that when people came to me for counseling they brought me their broken hearts and wounded spirits. I needed to learn how to meet them in the deep wound of their soul or spirit, how to care for this part of them. To do so with integrity, I needed to develop more of my own spiritual life. I had not been paying attention to this still, small voice so it had to grow louder to get my attention; eventually it burst into flame. I felt scorched. I was apprehensive leaving a known career and venturing into unknown territory. But I felt more alive than ever.

A Dark and Rainy Night

When we consciously think, feel, breathe, speak and act, we become the creators of our own lives. Months after the fire, when repairs to my house were finished, I saw an ad in a magazine that described a new spiritually oriented university in California. It sounded like the ideal program for me to learn more about the world's wisdom traditions and develop my spiritual practices. My mind told me I might become a better counselor; my heart told me I needed this for my own soul. I sent for information, loved the sound of the program and with great excitement filled out the application and sent it off. Weeks later I received a letter saying I had been accepted. Then reality set in. I had a grief-counseling career; my clients depended on me and expected me to be available. My wife and children needed me. This university was on the other side of the country. How could I afford the tuition costs and books? I wasn't sure that I could do all the reading and write the required papers. It would be expensive to fly out to California for classes. Where would I stay? I put the acceptance letter in a back corner of my desk. Several months later, I heard that the founder of the university, Matthew Fox, was coming to speak at a local church that we had attended occasionally. I remember the night well. It was a dark and rainy Friday, windy and chilly for a May evening. The church was full, with more people than I'd ever seen there before. Because of the stormy weather, Matthew's plane was late. A local singer and guitar player entertained us as we waited impatiently. I was eager and anxious. Finally Matthew arrived. Two hours later I turned to my wife with tears in my eyes and said, "I have to go." With tears in her eyes, she said, "You have to go." Looking back, I can see the progression of my journey since the fire had woken me up to the reality that my counseling career was better left behind, and that the spiritual realm was beckoning.

Ultimately, I had to listen to my inner voice. In two months, I flew to California and began studies at the University of Creation

Spirituality. Soon, as I discovered the riches of the world's wisdom traditions, I realized I wanted to be ordained as a minister. I entered a parallel program at an interfaith seminary. In both programs, I was exposed to many new spiritual practices. A teacher told a story of the Hindu sage Ramakrishna. When he was asked how he felt about his spiritual practice, he replied, "I feel like a fish released from a pot into the water of the Ganges." I felt similarly. I resonated deeply with the words of another of my teachers, modern mystic Andrew Harvey, who said, "The ultimate adventure is claiming complete responsibility for our own spiritual development." I agreed. Yet, I walked this new path tentatively. When we are novices with little understanding, as I felt, a state described by the idea of the Buddhist's "Beginner's Mind", it helps to know that when we enter into spiritual practice, we join those many people, ancient and modern, ancestors and neighbors, who have themselves embraced spiritual practice. Gradually, as I became more involved in my practices, I felt embraced by these people. Suddenly I was not alone, not separate in my despair, not separate in my ecstasy, but in communion, together with and part of a community of practitioners.

Some spiritual practices are private: solitary meditation or prayer, use of a mantra or the Rosary under our breath. We can imagine God inside us, beside us, or a field of white light around us. Some practices are public: when we sit with others in meditation, march in protest, serve food to the hungry, pray together in a church congregation. Any form of spiritual practice deepens us, as we wake up to change, inside and out. This sharpens the conviction, the deep knowing, that we are already that which never changes, the Eternal. For me, spiritual practice is like sitting under an endless waterfall that cleans and washes me, that melts away layer after layer until more and more of my essence is revealed.

Spiritual Practice: "Your Spiritual Companions"

Sit in a place of rest and silence; imagine that beings approach you, beings that become identifiable as they come closer. They join the deep silence and gather around you, gently and serenely. They smile and nod their heads with quiet greetings to each other and to you. Slowly, you understand that these new companions are ancient adepts, spiritual teachers, saints and sages from long ago. They are here to bring their wisdom and love to you. They softly mill around you, some make slow and gentle gestures of peace, and others offer graceful quiet blessings. Some sing or chant softly. Others simply stand quietly near you, elegant, calm and loving. You realize they are present in your life, now and always, as tender and supportive spiritual companions.

Chapter 10

Essence Through Meditation

Meditation:

Meditation, here and now, offers us a chance to gaze into our essence with the same tender passion of gazing into the eyes of our beloved.

Meditation is a process of purification, distillation, simplification and arrival at essence. To meditate is to create a time and space for silence and reflection. Deeper depths of Spirit are revealed; we don't know the source, we just know the depths are present in the mystery of not knowing. Meditation has these many layers, and an early layer is to listen to the thoughts and feelings that arise naturally. As we listen without judgment, we will hear what we think and what we feel. It's easy to say "without judgment". But what do we do when, indeed, the judgments arrive unbidden? They can choke up our space, flood our mind with negativity instead of love. First, we can harvest the insight. It can be interesting to see what shows up; we learn what our preferences are. Second, we have an opportunity to harvest the garbage for fruit. Notice the noise, judgments, the 'obscurations and obstacles'. With meditation practice, slowly, over time, this confusion and discomfort can quiet. These are but layers of habituation that have been ignored over time and have built up and been confused as the egoic self. This ignorance leads to attraction and aversion, as the Buddhists say, and they obscure essence. We can learn from what we are attracted to and what we avoid. Monkey mind happens. It will happen. When it does, after the illumination of the harvest, we can let the thoughts and feelings slide on through. We can give them grease so they will slip away. In Buddhism, these busy messages are disturbances that obscure our true nature of tranquility, luminosity and spaciousness.

Precisely because they can come, they can go. We need to keep that tiny thin slice at the top of our awareness of the present moment free and open so that the love available to us can arrive. (See Chapter 7: Awareness of Essence.) Meditation is a time to screen out distractions, internal and external, in order to find and experience our true nature under all the thoughts and feelings we have about our stories and wounds. Meditation can be a time of healing. The similarity between the words meditation and medicine is significant here, particularly because one definition of medicine – which we associate with healing – is 'ritual practice'. Meditation is a form of ritual spiritual practice.

Meditation Instructions

To create a meditation practice, establish a definite and repeated procedure over a period of time. It is similar to other practices that we build into everyday life, where the goal is to increase our skill level by familiarity and repetition. Like other practices, it helps to have a regular routine and a consistent physical place. However, meditation practice has a fundamental difference. Familiarity in meditation can breed expectation, which may lead us out of the present moment, the only place – and it's not a place – that true meditation can be experienced. Meditation practice is not an escape but a new event every time we sit on cushion or chair. Choose a comfortable physical posture that allows your body to be fully supported. Sit in a chair or or on a bench, or kneel or sit on a round cushion, often called a zafu. It is helpful to also have a foundation cushion, often square, called a zabuton, to support your legs and feet, especially if the floor is hard. Buttocks need to be higher than your legs and feet, which are in contact with the floor. This enables you to be in touch with the energy of the earth. Your back is straight so that energy can flow up and down. Your eyes can be lightly closed or holding a soft gaze to the floor in front of you. If you are distracted by the visual field, it is best to close your eyes. As your body settles in and relaxes, breathe through the nose and rest the tip of the tongue lightly on the roof of the mouth behind the front teeth, with lips soft. Expand your diaphragm as you inhale. Place your attention on the breath under the nostrils as it moves in and out. Notice when thoughts come and go in your mind. Breathing in, you might use a prompt like, "Ah, breath, there you are," and then breathe out and release sensations and distraction. Then, gently and without judgment, reapply the focus on the breath itself. You can feel your abdomen rising with the in-breath and falling with the out-breath. Up and down, in and out. Bring your breath all the way into your lungs, farther into your body and into your arms and legs. Then let it all the way out. Again and again.

It can be helpful to focus on something, such as the breath as it comes in and goes out, or a word or sound used as a mantra. But it is important not to try to *do* anything, or to resist or *undo* anything. The delicious key is simply to accept everything just as it is, here and now. No need to change anything, do anything, accomplish anything; this moment is what it is. The peace of acceptance is available.

Morning is a prime time to meditate because we are emerging from a period of sleep and silence, and we haven't yet encountered the coming day's worldly demands. As far as length of time goes, twenty to thirty minutes works well. Remember, quality of attention is more critical than quantity of content. However, consistency is also important, even if the time period is short; I've learned that the more I practice, the easier I can drop into a meditative state. To give yourself the gift of extended meditation time – days or weeks – is not only beneficial in and of itself, but it can also propel you deeper into your inner being. Meditation will illuminate your attractions and aversions. Call them what they are. To name them reduces their power, reduces their hold. This will allow you to deepen, reinvigorate and enliven your daily practice. At a deeper level, we do not seek any qualities such as peace or acceptance, we *are* these qualities. Thus there is no 'product' of meditation; the 'process' of meditation is effortless. I think of the Buddhist notion of least effort or right effort. The only work is to accept whatever is. And we don't have to make work of acceptance. We do have to take the time to offer meditation as a simple gift: a few minutes just for us. We do have to create the space in our life, we do have to walk into the room, and sit down. The rest can come as easily as we let it.

Most of us want to be available, engaged and helpful to our friends, family and at our work. We want to be awake and responsive. Yet, as I tell my students, "How can you listen to anyone else unless and until you can listen to yourself?" Welcome to meditation, where we finally sit as a listening witness to our self, and once we get beyond the distortions and distractions, we listen to our essence. Eventually we understand that we are addressing the ultimate question, "Who is this person who meditates, who am I?" Simply by asking this question, we become an observer. We create a valuable separation from all our thoughts, feelings and 'monkey-mind'. This is a valuable insight because now we realize we are not our thoughts and feelings; they come and they go, they arise in consciousness and they disappear from consciousness. We are human, so thoughts and feelings always come and always go. But what is stable and consistent is our very consciousness itself, the essential core of our being, our essence.

My Practice

I began to practice meditation 40 years ago. I got up early in the morning and walked over to the "Little Kids" building at Collins Brook School, a rural alternative school I started in 1969. I sat on the blue, sun-warmed carpet, very aware that in an hour six boisterous elementary students would come charging into the building. I soaked up the precious silent time. Since then, I have meditated with practitioners in Rashneeshpuram, Oregon, by myself on a Marin Headlands' cliff overlooking the Golden Gate Bridge in San Francisco, in solitude in a cabin on Great Duck Island, Maine, these last years in the Chaplaincy Institute of Maine classroom on Thursday mornings, or daily on my cushion at home. Each time I create anew a familiar comfort, relief and peace. Each time, my body and soul remember the peace and stability available, anytime, any place, no matter what else is going on. My meditation practice is a constant, regardless of where I am physically or emotionally.

The benefits of meditation are described in many ways: physical relaxation, emotional clarity, mental relaxation, peace of mind, relief from stress, spiritual growth, awakening and, yes, enlightenment. Yet, rather than trying to achieve something, like relaxation or peace, meditators come to realize and accept that these qualities already exist. They are present underneath the internal chatter and external distractions. All of the 'goals' of meditation – whatever they are – are always already available. Meditation provides the immediate possibility to accept and harvest what already is available. Yes, meditation requires a certain discipline, the intention to take a few moments to sit down, and be with yourself. And to let go of all those thoughts. Let go, let go.

I like having a definite, consistent physical place for everyday meditation. When I commit myself to meditation by walking into the room, I feel welcomed. The furnishings, temperature, light and space are familiar. I light incense to perfume the air. I remove my cushion from its storage space, and place it on the floor just where I like it. I sit on it facing my Buddha figure, who encourages me. I use a timer so that I do not have to be concerned with the distraction of keeping time. A soft bell begins and ends my practice. While I can and do meditate in other places, sometimes with other people, I have a home base, a home practice. It is a ritual I have created to maintain my practice. As the years have unfolded, I can meditate anywhere because it is the meditative state itself that is my real home, and I carry that with me wherever I go. Through the years, of course, I also carry around my chattering mind, the seemingly endless avalanche of thoughts and feelings hell-bent on disturbing my focus and serenity. When (not if) I experience these distractions, it does not mean that I have failed in my meditation, or my meditation practice, it simply gives me yet another opportunity to succeed, to bring my attention back to the meditative state, gently and without judgment. This coming back happens when I remember to focus on my breath, or on a word or brief phrase I might use as a mantra. A mantra is just that, an inner verbal visualization that serves to focus the mind. The Buddhists say a mantra is 'mind protection', or 'saving the mind'. A mantra is a word, phrase or sound expressive of the essence of life. It can be the sound of the Universe, 'Om'. For me, a mantra's repetition brings forth energy that is grounded in the earth, available to me as it vibrates in my chest and moves up and out my mouth. When I focus on my mantra, I am so intent on that word or phrase that nothing else can get in; my mind is protected. When my mind strays away from this protection, my mantra returns me to meditation like a signpost that points home. Possible words to use as a mantra are: 'peace', the name of a divine entity I relate to, or a Sanskrit phrase such as 'so hum', which means I am that, or 'sat, chit, ananda' which means existence, consciousness, bliss. For me, a mantra is like having a secure anchor when my boat is tossed about in the ocean storm of thoughts.

Hummingbird Meditation

On a visit to relatives in Michigan, I went outside early one morning and sat down beside a pond with a water fountain spraying water up into the still dawn sky. With my eyes closed in meditation, I listened to the sound of the water splashing back into the pond. I heard the rustle of the wind in the thin trees. Later, deep into meditation, I suddenly heard a different sound, up close, a steady whirring. I opened my eyes to see, right square in front of my face, an inch or so away, a hummingbird. It stayed right there, gazing intently into my eyes. I didn't move. Its small yellow eyes looked directly into mine. I shut my eyes again. Still, it remained there, motionless except for its whirring wings. I could feel the air from its wings on my face. A moment went by. Another. Breathing in and out. Meditation. Suddenly, the hummingbird flew away; the thrumming of its wings faded quickly into the sound of the falling water. I opened my eyes and saw it dart into the woods. It was gone. I closed my eyes, and felt the emptiness, then a new deeper stillness. I was left stunned, awakened anew, propelled deeper into my meditation, which I wanted to continue forever. I felt touched by a definite blessing, privileged to behold and receive a benediction from a small yet great beauty, which affirmed my place in the Universe.

Meditating Together

I like the common intention and group energy available from meditating with other people. The social and spiritual benefits of joining others to meditate can be substantial. When I joined 1000 other Rajneesh devotees for early morning meditation in Oregon, I would begin to enter a meditative state as soon as I awoke that day, knowing my intention for the morning. Groups of us walked the dusty road to the bus stop together. I felt the quiet camaraderie from our shared destination of meditation. We all knew where we were headed and there was little small talk. Together, we boarded the bus to take us to the mediation hall, which was immense, and decorated with colorful flowers and hanging banners. As I found a cushion and a place to sit, I felt surrounded by hundreds of friends. When I closed my eyes, these unknown friends remained very present. When we commit to showing up to meditate together, it is an expression of our longing for communion, our wish to share our essence through deeply held interconnection. No need for explanations or social talk. We are sharing something profound and meaningful just by being together in silent stillness. We share a belief that we are valued by each other not for our exterior but for our interior. During the shared stillness, our meditating companions share their presence in various involuntary ways, a cough here, a rustling of clothing there, offering their gifts. These gifts are two-fold. One gift is potential distraction so that we can remember to return to our meditation. This too we are sharing, the continuous coming back from our distractions. We are all vulnerable here with others: we are vulnerable together. The second gift is the rustlings, sighs and audible breathing that show that many other people are present with us. When we meditate together, we experience direct evidence that we are not alone in our practice.

As individual and internal as meditation is, we benefit from companions, their energy, intention and practice. Even when they are not present physically, to know that friends meditate is helpful and supportive. These days, meditation is worldwide, common among many religions and spiritual practices. It is therefore a bond among all peoples, a powerful and peaceful, even peace-creating, communion. Every time we sit, we create a precious present and a precious promise of unity. Our meditation is a conversation with Spirit. We listen to our essence.

Spiritual Practice: "Meditation"

Whether or not you have ever meditated before, for right now, here, as you read these words, prepare to meditate anew, as if for the first time in your life. For, in a very real way, this moment *is* brand new. Sit erect though comfortable. Allow the chair, cushion or floor to support you, and know that these in turn are supported by the earth. Mother Nature herself holds you. Breathe in and out with a new consciousness and appreciation for the energy given to you. As your body settles in and relaxes, notice your thoughts as they come and go in your mind. Remember you have a mind to use, but you are not your mind.

Let the thoughts come, and let the thoughts go. They come in, they go out. Thoughts flow in and out like a stream flowing down its streambed. Simply be with that flow, that movement, that smooth steady motion, the natural way water finds its course gently downhill. Rest in the quiet knowledge of knowing that eventually all water reaches the ocean.

Chapter 11

Essence Prayer

Meditation:
The silence we feel now is not an intermediary space between ourselves and Spirit, but the exact space where we join Spirit.

Prayers are conversations with Spirit, the word I am using to describe all the other various names for God the Creator, the Holy One, Essence. Prayers are two-way communications, essence to essence. To speak or to imagine words is only one dynamic; to listen is the crucial second dynamic. Spirit 'speaks' to us in many ways. We may hear literal words from the Divine, inside our heads, and from other people whom the Divine is using as spokespeople. These could be recognized religious leaders or spiritual teachers, or the neighbor next door, or animals, or the trees, bushes and flowers of the natural world. It is equally true that God, Spirit, communicates, prays with us, in myriad forms other than words, forms as many and varied as God herself, as Creation himself. As many faith traditions tell us, whatever we name this, it is very often found or revealed in silence.

I sat quietly on my back-yard deck early in the summer morning and heard bird songs, and watched the first sunlight turn golden the fragile quivering leaf tips of the tall oak trees far overhead. Are these not gifts from the Creator of a precious new day? Prayer begins as simply a wish to connect with the Divine. Such a wish may stem from peace or from desperation. Prayer is an intention to be in connection with the Holy Spirit. Yet, to define our praying to Spirit inherently posits a duality: I am praying over here, communicating with Spirit, which is over there. Let's melt that duality and suppose that we are not separate. Or, at least, let's remember that while we may start out being separate, or feeling separate, we may create a process, or a path, that will lead us away from separateness, toward communion and unity. Our dilemma, or perhaps it is our grace, is that even while we long for the Divine, we are always already in its presence. Prayer is more accurately, and actively, a way we strengthen, deepen, expand, cultivate and nurture that very connection, the very unity that exists now, here, everyday.

Common and Available

Prayer commonly begins as thought. Because we are human, we think. Our minds create endless thoughts. To step into the responsibility of owning and directing our own thoughts – being mindful – is to create a powerful shift: we can use and direct what we are already doing, thinking, to make our lives prayerful, literally full of prayer. Since we are already thinking, it is but a valuable shift of consciousness to give our thinking purpose and direction. With this new consciousness, any stimulus from our interior thoughts or our outside environment can be a call to prayer, a call to be in relationship with the Divine, to be connected to Spirit. Imagine how life can change when we are constantly called to be in communion with God, to be God's companion, essence to essence. Imagine, nay, *remember* when we listen and respond affirmatively to such a call! What if this call encouraged us to pray as naturally as to breathe? When I feel lost and lonely, simply to remember that I can pray is lifesaving. Suddenly I am no longer alone, for as I begin to pray I realize that by doing so, in fact simply by having the wish or intention to pray, I am in that very instant joining everyone in all of human history who has ever prayed. And this is deeply comforting.

Prayer is quickly and easily available, any place, any time, under any circumstance. It can be found and expressed in any of the Four Quadrants described previously: body/physical, heart/emotional, mind/intellectual/mental and soul/spiritual. We pray with our bodies when we offer our physical self to God. This is called embodied prayer, and can take forms such as Yoga, dance, walking, swimming or simply placing our arms and hands in an attitude of prayer. We can pray with our emotional self, expressing our natural emotions to God, such as anger or sadness, or love. Our tears of grief – sharing our sadness with Spirit – can be expressions of prayer. We can pray with our mind, our intellect, when we bring to mind a prayerful image, or remember words from scripture. We can pray with our spiritual self, when we acknowledge that our expressions of prayer are not bound by time or space. Just as we saw that health can be defined as a balance among the Four Quadrants, to engage all of them indicates a healthy prayer life. In these ways, prayer expresses all parts of a person. Prayer can collect our often-scattered selves and connect them together, and promote balance and integration. A primary purpose of prayer is exactly that: connection, communion and unity, both with our deepest selves and with that which is beyond and beneath ourselves, the transcendent, the Divine.

Several years ago, I wanted to encourage grieving families, and gently suggest to them that they were not as alone as they sometimes felt, and that a source of strength might be found in prayer. I wrote the following words for them, which now stand in the entryway to the Center for Grieving Children. I also read this at every training session for new volunteer facilitators of grief groups.

Meditation Prayer for the Center for Grieving Children
May the grieving children, and their families
Who enter these doors
Find here a new kind of home,
Or perhaps an old kind of home,
Created by people who ourselves
Know tears and anger and love.

We create this home anew
Every night the stars come out,
Every day the sun shines,

Though clouds may hide the light:
Those old stars have been in our sky for over 10 billion years,
That old sun has been in our sky for over a billion years.
And will be tonight,
And will be today.

Birds have been here for 150 million years,
Cats and dogs have been here for 36 million years.
When we came, 2.5 million years ago,
We began loving,
We began grieving.

And we are grieving still, tonight and today,
Here in our new home,

Where tears are welcome,
Where anger is welcome,
Where love is welcome,
Where you are welcome.

The simple words "Let us pray" can be both revolutionary and healing. Suddenly Spirit, God, a Presence – call it what you will – is welcomed into the room, and a space for reverence is created. Suddenly, sometimes against all odds, we are not alone, but newly in communion with a Source that was absent before the intention was thought or spoken. Now it is present. Any person can speak the intention to pray or call for Spirit. A challenging or painful circumstance, suffering, calls for a person with presence who in that moment can be a new leader who has the presence of mind – really, presence of heart – to be aware of what is needed and create comfort, healing, or peace. This person does not have to be a recognized clergy member. The moment calls for – the Divine is calling for – someone to step forward, to hear the need, heed the call for prayer, and thus remember and re-create in the present moment the natural state and the experience of unity, communion, a prayerful state.

Natural Prayer Circle

As a volunteer with the Center for Grieving Children, I received a call from the local high school principal. She called the day after an 11th grade student named Josh had fallen out of the back of a friend's pickup truck, hit his head on the pavement and died. She said the accident had happened a block from school when the students were on their lunch break, and now the students were distraught. She wanted to know how to help them. I arranged to meet with three of Josh's friends at the high school. We sat together in a small office with all the noise and activity of a normal school day outside in the hallway. The students were sad and red-eyed. They didn't have much to say, but I listened. After they told me a little bit about Josh, they said they wanted to have a memorial for him. They wanted it at the street corner where he died, and they wanted it now. We went to see the principal, and thankfully she agreed to use the school's public address system to announce that there would be a memorial service for Josh at the lunch break in half an hour. The students and I walked over to the street corner. Soon other students began arriving. There was a little sand sprinkled on the spot in the street where Josh had died the day before, and students gathered in a ragged circle around it. Nobody said anything. We stood in silence. The feeling was reverential and prayerful; we were just there together. Then, out of the corner of my eye, I saw two TV sound trucks drive up, followed by a police cruiser. I glanced at the kids and they looked nervous; some pointed at the TV crew getting out of their trucks. I quickly walked over to the police officers as they got out of their car and asked them to keep the TV people away. The officers looked at the kids, then they walked over and motioned to the TV crews to move their cameras away. Then the officers put up traffic barriers to protect the street from cars. By now about 50 or so kids were standing in the circle, and they watched all this. Soon one student said, "Well, I guess we should say stuff about Josh." So they did. Around the circle, when they were moved to speak, they spoke about Josh. Their words, and how they said them, were sad, truthful, profane, funny and touching. Their voices were soft, choked-up, loud, angry, grieving and full of loss and truth. His girlfriend sat on the curb, right beside the flowers that someone had placed in the exact spot where Josh died. She was bent over with her head in her arms, crying. Her friends comforted her. Eventually, people stopped speaking and silence returned. Then, without another word, they drifted away, back to school or home. The students knew what to do and they knew how to do it; they came together to remember their friend Josh. They made it happen and they participated. They prayed with their bodies by showing up, they prayed with their words by being truthful and reverent, they prayed with their silence by letting it be. Everything they said and did spontaneously felt, to me, like prayer. I was astounded and heartened by the kids and their innate knowing what they needed for themselves. The experience was precious and also fragile; protection was called for, as well as attendance. Prayer is both that simple, all around us, and that intentional. The result is both powerful and healing.

Two Prayers

(I wrote these prayers when I was a Chaplain on visits to hospital and hospice patients. I would often leave written prayers on bedside tables, or posted up on the wall where the patient and his or her visitors could see them, and thus be reminded that I had visited.)

Heavenly Father, Earthly Mother, Gracious God of All:
We reach out to you as the Creator
of every minute of our lives.
Let us open our hearts to receive the healing Love you shower
   upon us.
May we know the deep truth of your
Compassionate and Generous Spirit
as it awakens divine healing in us.
Blessed be. Amen.

Oh Holy One, God, Great Spirit, Thank you for this precious
   time to be with each other, and with You.
We pray that You might hold our fragile bodies and tender
   souls in your strong and protective arms.
Thank you.

Corn Ceremony

When I was a student at the University of Creation Spirituality in
California, I took a course on Native traditions, taught by Jose
Hobday, a Seneca elder and Franciscan nun, born of a Seneca-
Iroquois mother and a Southern Baptist father. She told us stories
of her Seneca matrilineal culture, and then directed us to make
prayer sticks. Early that morning on my walk in a neighborhood
park, I had found a branch that had fallen from a cypress tree. In
class I attached four strips of colored cloth to it: red, yellow,
white and black, to represent the earth-centered four directions
from Native traditions: South, East, North and West. Jose
described the late-summer harvest festival celebrated by her
extended family, the native ritual to express gratitude to Spirit
for the harvest of sufficient food to make it through another
winter. Then she handed out kernels of corn, symbols of the
harvest, and led us in a prayer to bless the corn with our new
prayer sticks as thanksgiving for an abundant crop. Her resonant
voice filled the city classroom, bringing her people's earth-based

tradition to life. Then, carrying our prayer sticks and corn, we walked down the stairs and outside to the Oakland streets and to the parkway in front of the school building. Our class of twelve students separated and walked individually onto the wide grassy median. Slowly and reverently we scattered the corn kernels in the thin brown grass. We blessed the whole area with our prayer sticks. We prayed for peace and healing for Oakland's harsh urban environment, and tried to convey the spirit of the Native American harvest ritual. We finished and walked back upstairs to the classroom. Suddenly we heard sirens outside. In our classroom again, we watched from the windows. The sirens grew louder and louder. Looking down into the street, we saw many police cars, with their blue lights flashing, drive slowly by, right along the parkway where we just had blessed the grass median with the corn kernels and our prayer sticks. Someone told us that two police officers had been shot and killed earlier that week, and that this was the procession of police cruisers and fire trucks on their way to the funeral service. The families, friends and fellow officers of the slain police would unite in their grief and thanksgiving for the lives of their loved ones. Now they were driving through the exact space we had just blessed. Suddenly, in a way that now is always with me, I understood that anytime I hear sirens of any kind, I hear them as a call to prayer, a call to send prayers to police officers, firefighters, EMTs, ambulance drivers, patients, and accident victims. In this way, my understanding and use of prayer has been transformed and expanded.

The word for pray in Aramaic can mean to incline or bend toward, listen to, or lay a snare for. We lay a snare with our devotion, and sometimes our raw and desperate need, and hope to catch some inspiration, solace or connection with the Divine. The Hebrew roots of the word pray also suggest the image of a bottomless depth or cavern, or the shadow or shade created by a canopy, roof, or veil. These images portray the depth and spaciousness that prayer creates. When we pray, we open a space for sacred connection. And again comes that ultimate question, who exactly is it seeking connection, doing the praying? Are we not a mirror of the Divine? Contemplating this is itself a daily prayer practice that can express our essence.

Spiritual Practice: "My Praying People"

Find a quiet space and time when you can enter a relaxed state of prayer. Stand with your feet comfortably supporting you. Imagine yourself in a large and safe space. It might be a space you know, that you like to visit, a beach, a meadow or a forest. Or you can create such a space right now in your mind. Feel yourself standing securely in this place. Now imagine that you are standing as part of a large circle of prayerful beings, old and young, ancient and contemporary, that slowly and gently materialize around you. They come to be with you here and now, as if they step quietly out from the mists of time. You realize that these are all the people who have ever prayed before, anyone and everyone who has ever asked for help, anyone who has ever lifted a broken heart or wounded soul up to the heavens seeking solace, assistance, comfort and healing. They gather quietly around you, beside you, all clearly in a state of prayer. You know they are praying with you and for you. With deep gratitude, you join them silently in prayer, in profound spiritual communion. Eventually these beings slowly melt away and you stand in your essence, completely filled with their ceaseless prayers, and filled with a new sense of connection.

Chapter 12

Essence Art

Meditation:
Though the Great Silence is always already available underneath everything, it takes the artful creator of your life to turn the eye of the needle just so to accept your unique thread.

Art is creative expression that can illuminate and activate our essence. My definition of art includes any and every form of art and artistic expression. Some of these are music, dance, poetry, printmaking, sculpture, theater, photography, painting, writing and drawing. Emotional passion has long inspired art, and art in turn has been a primary means to express the emotions of religious and spiritual beliefs and practices. Whether we engage with it as creator, participant or viewer, art is a powerful way to access and activate the spiritual realm. Also, art is a primary practice to create sacred space, space for worship, meditation, prayer and religious ritual. Art of any sort is an expression of our interior, what we think, what we feel, and at the deepest level, an expression of our essence. Certainly, to speak at all is to artfully choose words, which we then form into a sentence or a phrase or a paragraph of expressed thought that we share with another person. When there are no words, or conversely, too many words, making art can give our soul's expression not in verbal form, but visual, or sculptural, etc. Many of us do not think of ourselves as artists, but we all have souls, and our souls are longing for expression. We all have an inner artist able to create and express aspects of our soul. While art is a powerful tool to express the soul, it is also the means by which the soul is communicated to another person who is engaging with the artistic expression. Making art drops us down under the thinking mind, the intellectual brain, into the territory of instinct, intuition, primal creativity. Everything we do, everything we are, can be an art form, even to look with our eyes and speak with our voice. The quality of our feelings when we look into another's eyes, and when we speak to them, is our essence displayed, a kind of immediate art in the precious present moment. As we become more conscious of this, of ourselves as artists, the world will become more conscious and beautiful.

Painting

When I was about twelve years old, I was annoyed and frustrated by my two younger sisters and brother. My parents were giving them important things such as bicycles and a book on sexuality, years younger than when I had been given them, and I didn't think it was fair. Something inside me felt violated, but I couldn't express my hurt and anger in words. I found some old bed sheets and tacked them up on a basement wall. I took the leftovers of my father's house paints and with a big brush I splattered paint on the sheets, letting it slide and drip down the sheet in rivers of color and form. I loved that I did not have to explain my feelings in words; I didn't have any words. And besides, if I did have words, the words I'd choose wouldn't be OK to express in my family. But I could paint what I felt; I could whip the brush around, and slash the paint any way I wanted. After the big paintings dried, I brought them upstairs and hung them in my room. When, some years later, I learned about Jackson Pollock, I felt more affirmed. I loved looking at the graceful and explosive colors – red, orange, black, purple – dotting, dripping, dancing down the hanging cloth. That was me up there, my anger, my frustration, my excitement, parts of me I didn't know I had inside, now outside, alive, in new and colorful expression.

My senior year of high school I was floundering, bored with the traditional courses, closed in by the snowy New Hampshire winter, trapped in the cold and musty wooden-walled classrooms of the old prep school. I needed a half-credit to graduate, and I impulsively enrolled in a studio-painting course. The class began, and I discovered that in addition to the class time, students had access to the art studio anytime they wanted. So I came in nights after supper and early on weekend mornings. The rich, earthy smell of oil paint hung heavy and delicious in the spacious painting room. The high-ceilinged space was flooded from above with abundant winter light. Half-finished paintings sat in a circle, like ghosts around the empty model's platform. The atmosphere invited me to bring a new and deeper part of myself forward, unknown as it was. In silence, I stood in front of my wooden easel that held a blank canvas. I allowed an inner intuition that did not have words to come up and out along my arm, and into my fingers to the paintbrush. I dipped my brush into the bright red, the deep blue, and the other vibrant colors that were about to speak for me. I moved the brush across the empty white canvas. I could not have done this with my classmates or the art teacher in the room; I needed solitude. I felt empty making my first tentative strokes, as if something valuable was leaving me. I worried that I wasn't going to find a creative spark, but that was only what I thought I should feel. Images began to appear in front of me on the canvas. Then the very emptiness itself emerged, in color and form. The paint smoothed, splattered and dripped with a life of its own. I realized I had a new tool, painting, to literally see myself more clearly, on the canvas. What I saw was both form and formless, seen and unseen, and beautiful.

One painting showed a dark empty tenement room, with cracked and peeling wall plaster, and a high dirty broken window, opening to a narrow alley outside. By a frayed cord, a single light bulb hung from the ceiling. It was unlit, an expression of my struggle with creativity. The second painting was more abstract, portraying two stylized alien-like figures who sat, cross-legged, facing each other in silence. There it was: my yearning for relationship, not knowing how to create anything except the abstract people sitting close but not touching or interacting in any way. They were present but alien to each other, flat, unmoving and silent. This was just the way I felt with people, certainly alien and frustrated and lonely, in between youth and maturity, caught in a high school world I had just finally figured out and scared of what came next. I was elated that, even in this time of uncertainty, I had discovered new tools to encounter and express what I experienced. I didn't even know if I wanted to go to college, which was the expected course. But all my friends were going, and my teachers and parents expected me to go.

Transition

I felt lost in the middle of all the transitions, leaving the known life of high school, and entering the unknown. My painting changed. I became fascinated by the boundaries of things, where two different forms and colors – or people – met, and substances interacted with each other, melted together and transformed into something entirely different and new. Or the two edges kept their boundaries and shapes, colors and qualities, coexisting, relating but still separate. As spring came, and the snow began to melt, I walked by the pond in back of my dormitory. I would kneel on the shoreline and watch the cold muddy water meet and melt the thin translucent ice crystals from the pond. I photographed these images with my mind and took them into the painting studio. I painted this communion of two different substances, muddy water and ice crystals. Painting became my reason for getting up in the morning. I'd paint one color, a dark brown, then add red, then yellow, then change my brush stroke and add green, white, and then a thin purple. I would watch the paint pigment, sometimes thick, sometimes a thin wash, blend and slowly fuse together as a new color, a new form. I let the paint have its own way on the canvas. I picked up the canvas and turned it back and forth so the paint ran wherever it wanted to go in decreasing rivulets. Sometimes I added threads and bits of cloth, which altered the streams of paint and gave the painting texture, a new dimension. I saw and loved the beauty in randomness. I understood better that nature did indeed have its own course. This was a needed antidote and a possible solution to the pressures I felt from the prep school and my parents, the imperative to make decisions about college. I could see new possibilities to take time, allow more space and silence. The secure boundary, the persona I had created to survive high school, was changing. I wasn't sure how much of it, if any, would be useful in college. There it all was in front of me, in form, with its own beauty, for me to contemplate. I thought that maybe I could go to an art school, instead of one of the liberal arts colleges my parents expected me to attend. But every time I brought that possibility up with them, they would say I could do that after I went to a 'real' college. I could see the handwriting on the wall; I wasn't going to an art school. When I did enroll at an Ivy League University, during the first semester I chose several paintings to hang in a student show. When someone offered to buy one, I felt affirmed but I wasn't ready to let go of it; it was too personal to share with the public. I decided to keep it. It is in my workshop today.

Years later, when my wife was in the hospital recovering from surgery, I painted a large hanging banner to bring to her room. I wanted to give her something of my presence when I couldn't be there physically. I used shelf paper, about two feet wide, and five feet tall. Spontaneously, without much thought, I concentrated on choosing colors I knew she would like. I painted a big rambling green vine growing up out of brown soil, blooming into bold yellow flowers. Early the next morning, I came into her hospital room while she was still asleep and hung it up at the foot of her bed. It was the first thing she saw when she woke up. I saw her eyes move slowly to focus on the painting. She turned and looked at me and tears filled her eyes. She studied the painting and then asked me if I knew how many flowers were on the vine I had painted. I didn't so I looked. She pointed out that the vine had eleven flowers, the exact number of years we had been married. I smiled and my own tears came. The creative process had spoken with clarity and force, gave me a new confidence to trust my artistic intuition.

Enso Circles

I offer here one example of using art to identify and express essence: painting Enso Circles. Enso circles are an ancient Japanese art form that blends art and religion. While these circles are thought of as Buddhist, in fact they have origins in several wisdom traditions, including Hindu, Buddhist and Tao, making them interfaith in character. Painting Enso circles is a spiritual practice, sometimes done daily for decades. Typically, the circle is painted by the artist in one breath with a single stroke of the brush. Circles are found in many natural forms: the sun and moon, the planets, cells, bubbles, many flowers and plants. They remind us of completeness, of beginning and ending all in one form. The image of a circle represents the wholeness of the Universe available in the present, and the wholeness of life and death cycles. Circles suggest and give expression to serenity and completeness, the whole. Where is the beginning, the end? Painting Enso circles is an expression of spirit that transcends technique because the artist consciously paints in a meditative state. The process predominates. For me, this discipline begins with a creative trance. I paint one Enso circle, then continue in meditation to paint another, then another. Every circle is perfect. There is no 'right way' or 'artistically correct' circle. The process, how it's done, what we experience as the creator, is transformative too. For we are the artist of our soul, not just the artist of a product. Something is created out of nothing. In fact, if the paint were invisible paint so that it disappeared after drying on the paper, the result would be just as valuable.

The artist, in an act of courage, willingly confronts the

emptiness of the blank paper: nothingness. The instant the brush touches the paper, or the pen hits the page, out of nothing comes something. That something is essence, flowing from the artist's interior, a deep soulful place of infinite possibility. The possibility of beauty becomes probability, becomes inevitability, and then becomes creation. Creation of an Enso circle is akin to a personal Big Bang, the original creation of everything, nothing less. To own that responsibility is to step into our right, even our duty, to create life, to be an artist who is creating his or her life moment to moment, again and again, perfect circle after perfect circle.

As we create, we become the architects of change; we begin by destroying the tranquil empty surface of the paper. This creation brings the consequent inevitability of loss and grief, for everything changes. The instant my brush touches it, the blank empty space, the canvas or paper, is no longer empty. Something is lost. The new circle emerges, becomes whole as a new creation. Yet as finished as it appears, it too will change. It looks different as the light changes, as the perspective shifts. Holding the paper at a new angle brings a new awareness, a new perspective. Eventually, years later, the paper will age and the ink or paint will fade. Some day the painting will return to the earth from which it came. This is reflection of the Buddhist teaching of impermanence.

Rick

When my friend Rick, who was a sculptor, was in the hospital to receive treatment for serious cancer, I went to visit him. It turned out he was out of his room for some medical tests so I had a chance to hang up an Enso circle banner I had painted for him. I remembered that his room had a particular type of dropped-tile ceiling and I bought special hooks to fit the ceiling braces. I hung the Enso banner carefully where he could see it from his bed. When he returned from his tests and saw the banner, he smiled. He knew without me saying that I had painted it for him, out of my love and appreciation. We felt the bond of artists, and the artist's passion to transform space, to bring a new perspective and perhaps a new beauty. We knew the exciting possibilities of creativity, especially when and where it is least expected. Sharing art reminded us we had a long history of friendship, and friends making art. It was as if sharing our art together confirmed our inner knowing that there was more to our friendship than this hospital room, than his cancer. Without needing to say it out loud, we confirmed that we loved each other. We had hiked on Monhegan Island and delivered a joint sermon for the small community church there. Rick sculpted wild bears and tigers out of big chunks of wood. To this day, one of his sculptures, a yellow and black cheetah in the shape of a kid's chair, sits in the waiting room of my chiropractor. Soon after my hospital room visit, Rick left the hospital because no more treatments were available to him. He moved back home to be with his family for the Christmas season. He died three days after Christmas. In my sadness, I felt my bond with Rick continue in the days following his death. His wife, his friends and I designed his memorial service, which I facilitated a month later. I brought an Enso circle to his service as reminder to those present, and to me, of the endless circle of life and death.

Instructions for Painting Enso Circles

Here are directions for painting Enso circles as a simple form of spiritual practice. To begin, there is no right way to paint them. In an important way, they paint themselves. They arise out of our meditation. The process is of more value than the product. Or, the product *is* the process. I suggest you read these instructions through twice, then put the book down. First, allow yourself to receive: read the instructions. Then, after you have prepared the materials and meditated, allow yourself to express: paint the first circle. Because to paint Enso Circles is a meditation, art as meditation, or meditation as art, we begin with an intention to create sacred space and time, or time out of time, using the initial meditation. This is certainly time out of your day, an hour or more of uninterrupted time, without the usual distractions. Everything you do now counts: how you breathe, move, think, feel and respond to the continuing input from your five senses and your intuition, especially your intuition. As you settle into this time and space, please know that even how you create and arrange your workspace is significant. This, too, is an expression of your art as much process as product. Notice and appreciate the flat surface and available light. Gather the paint (or ink) and water, the brush, and the paper. I suggest that for Enso painting you have multiple sheets of paper available, at least 20 or more, so that you can continue to paint one circle after another. Choose or cut sheets of paper sized about 4" x 6" or 5" x 7". Mix the paint so that your brush stroke results in a firm black circle of paint that flows easily but doesn't clump. I suggest basic black acrylic, thinned slightly with water. Later on, I suggest you experiment with colors, but it's best to begin with the strength and simplicity of black. When you use colors, note that as your brush moves around the circle, the colors will tend to blend. I suggest you let the first colors dry a little, then use the additional colors. This will help maintain the purity of each color. Of course, you will have to stay in a meditative state longer, too, an added challenge and benefit. You can paint some test circles, but then we have to laugh because all our circles are tests! All our circles are complete as they are. When your materials are ready, stand or sit in front of your paint and paper. Close your eyes. Bring your awareness to how you stand, posture your body, and hold the brush. Even while there is no 'right' way, how you hold the brush and how you turn or twist the brush as you move it around making the circle will have an impact on the forms you create. Remember that to paint Enso circles, like all art creation, is to value the process as much or more than the product. Feel the support of the floor in your feet and legs, or the chair under you, giving you the strength and abundance of Mother Earth. Feel the air and sky above you, giving you the freedom and openness of Father Sky. Breathe easily. With each in-breath you take in the creative energy of the Universe, and with each out-breath you let go of what you no longer need. You are vanquishing any obstacle to creativity. This consistent cycle of regeneration of energy is yours to use now as you find your artistic essence inside. It is that still, small voice, perhaps a flickering feeling, of pure you. Breathe into this spark, and give it more life, as you would blow gently on an ember to turn it into flame and fire. Feel its warmth.

Open your eyes and with a soft gaze look down at the empty space in front of you. See the paper waiting. Consciously breathe in and breathe out. When you are ready, or even if you are not ready, actively bring forth your essential energy, from your heart center to your shoulder and down your arm into your wrist, hand and fingers to the brush. Dip it into the paint. Pause, and take in a deep breath. Now, in one motion without stopping, draw your first circle. Typically, I begin with a broad stroke on the left and move up, to the right and then down to finish with a thinner stroke close to the beginning. But, your circle will create itself, and each one is perfect *as it is*. That's the point. Honor and celebrate the circle you just created as perfect, so that you do not go back and 'correct' anything. There is nothing to correct. It is perfect as it is. Allow yourself to see and accept with your eyes and your heart the image that appears on the paper in front of you. Feel gratitude for Creation and your creation. Pause. Mindfully, choose another piece of paper, meditate again, and paint another circle in the same manner: one breath, one stroke, allowing it to emerge from you, to have a new unique life of its own. Paint another circle. Another, until you have used up all the paper. Before you put away your materials, reflect on the new Enso circles arrayed in front of you. Find a way to give thanks for your creativity, for these expressions of your essence. With appreciative eyes, breathe in the existence of the new circles shining there before you.

Additional suggestions: have a lot of paper available and paint quickly – more quickly than you would have 'planned'.

I have painted Enso circles measuring as small as an inch on paper, card-stock and wood, and as large as two feet on paper and cloth; and large single Enso circles on cloth banners 3' x 12'; these large banners have created sacred spaces by hanging inside and outside classrooms, churches and meeting halls. Once, when I arrived at my school office early one winter morning, I saw that the parking lot was empty, and that a fresh white layer of new snow covered it. I drove my car around in a big circle, to create an Enso circle in the newly fallen snow. Up in my office, I looked out the window and down to the black tire marks that formed a circle probably 60 feet across.

The consciousness brought forth by art as meditation, whether it is creating Enso circles or any other kind of art, serves to enhance our awareness and expression of our deepest selves. Art provides countless avenues of externalization, expanding us out into the world. The effect is two-fold. We see our formerly inner selves with more clarity and depth. And in this process of both creation and encounter, the world sees us. We are more known both to our world, and to ourselves. A sacred communion occurs. Certainly this is a lifelong process, made easier when we accept and bring forth the artist within, and when we recognize that our essence is longing for expression as the years of our lives unfold. Then we know it is an engaging and enlivening match, art and essence.

Spiritual Practice: "I Am an Enso Circle"

From the circles you have painted choose one that calls to you, or choose a circle from another source, such as nature. Center the circle in front of you. Next, imagine that this circle not only represents you, but *is* you, your spirit, your essence. Now describe the circle as if it were you yourself, using "I" statements. Examples:

"I am strong at the beginning then get narrow and graceful." "My definite black boundary protects a spacious interior." "I'm thick and strong all the way around." "My edges where I meet the world are thin and wobbly." Speak out loud or write down how you are an Enso Circle.

Chapter 13

Essence Beloved Community

Meditation:
When I am still, and you are still,
We are one stillness together.

After all this reading, all this work to understand ourselves, to heal ourselves, to be compassionate to ourselves, after all this longing to find our essence, we realize this is lonely work. One night, the moon is out at 3am shining in the window and down on our lone countenance. Now, knowing more than ever that no one can lead a life of essence for us, the loneliness sets in. And yet, I am not the only one. As we saw in the practices of meditation and prayer, as soon as we sit down, and soften our gaze, we are not alone. I join with spiritual teachers and mystics ancient and modern to say that we never have been alone, and we will never be alone. Even dying, 'alone' in the desert, or far out at sea, we are never alone. Eventually, like it or not, we feel others around us, our beloved community.

AIDS

In the early days of the AIDS epidemic, Frannie Peabody, whose grandson had developed AIDS, and other concerned people, came together to start The AIDS Project. At age 80, she was a tireless and outspoken advocate for providing AIDS support services such as HIV testing, medical treatment, and emotional and spiritual counseling. Back then, Maine families were faced with very sick sons moving back to Maine for end of life care. Inspired by Frannie's fierce dedication and compassion, we rented a small office space in a residential building in downtown Portland. We planned support groups for people living with HIV and their friends and family members. Though we knew it would be helpful for people who were trying to locate us, because we were worried about harassment we decided not to put up a sign. The night of the first group we had a snowstorm, but I was determined to get to the office. I drove downtown and found a parking place. I unloaded the wooden easel board I used to teach the natural emotions brought on by the fear of HIV illness and death. Because the office had no sign, I clambered up and down the snowy street searching for the address before I finally found the right building. Only two people showed up that night, but we had begun. We were part of a reluctant community, but a community nonetheless. We affirmed that in the face of intolerance we could create safety. We lived among ignorance, but we could create healing, if not always physically, then emotionally and spiritually.

I remember when I sat beside the hospital bed of a young man who was dying of AIDS. He was lying sunk into his bed, unconscious, scarcely breathing. The room was dim and quiet. I leaned forward and strained to hear his breath going in and out. I found that the rhythm of my breathing naturally began to match his. I said prayers quietly. I thanked God for his life, and asked for peace for his passing. All of a sudden he sat upright in the bed, raised his arms and stretched out his hands. His eyes did not open, yet his face shone with a soft light. In a weak raspy voice coming up from the deep essence of himself, he called out the names of his family members and a few friends. Then he lay back down, took several more breaths and stopped breathing. The room suddenly had more light. It came not from the window or the overhead, but from everywhere. I remained in the bedside chair and stayed there for a while. I felt alone but not lonely. I felt surrounded by light and love.

Months later, at the AIDS Day memorial service, I stood in the high wooden pulpit of the old stone Unitarian Universalist church in downtown Portland. These were early days of the

AIDS epidemic, when understanding and compassion were scarce. The people living with AIDS, their friends, families and caregivers were a newly bonded community, gathered together to remember and grieve those we had already lost, and were now losing. Many of the families and caregivers sat in front of me. A minister and then an AIDS Project staff member spoke. Then the Police Chief stepped up to speak. We felt fortunate he was willing to advocate for tolerance and acceptance; his support enlarged and strengthened our community. When it came my turn, I spoke of our new community and how we came together to hear our stories, and share our natural emotions, to share our suffering. A year or two later, when the AIDS Quilt came to another local church, we silently walked the aisles between the colorful panels, then read the names of those who had died. In that personal ritual, we not only came together again as a community, but also included those who were no longer with us in physical form, our larger community across time and space. Our loved ones, past and present, right here and over there on the other side of the veil, are our dear and present companions. For me, when I remember them, they are still with me. Their form is very different, but the memory itself is something real, an indication that the person, in spirit, is available, is still part of our community. Some essence is still present. That is so now, as we walk this earth, day-to-day, night-to-night and that is so always. And every year, especially on World AIDS Day, we remember them. I am honored to be a part of this beloved community.

Authentic Community

Many of us have a deeply human wish, a longing, to belong to a community of souls where we feel safe and secure. We long to be our true selves, show our natural emotions, live authentic lives, and live not only free of judgments, but also deliciously affirmed by others for being who we really are. No pretense, just essence. Before we are able to create this beloved community, or even accept the communities we are a part of already, it helps to make peace, or at least working agreements, with the various interior parts of ourselves that clamor for attention. This is our inner community of social roles along with their rules. We can ask permission from our Controller, our Judge, our Victim, our Caretaker, Our Seeker, our Follower, our Finder, our Wise Sage, our Innocent Child, our Skeptic, and our Fearful Self, among others. Quite a crowd! We can then enter a series of negotiations (with self and others) to leave the role-playing of the Victim Triangle behind and to inhabit our more healthy and authentic selves, that is, to live from within. We want to live from our essence.

This inner work to find and define our authentic self beyond social roles is the foundation for any true community. A community is a conscious collection of individuals bonded by intention. With the intention to join together comes the need to be humble, which comes from the word humus and means 'from the earth'. Here is another community. We are all living on the earth, and we share this space and time as we reconnect our individual selves with the earth under our feet, breathe in the sweet air around us. We summon up the courage to accept and forgive others who might be in our community. We especially need to accept ourselves and forgive ourselves so that we feel worthy of being members of a community. This is the prerequisite work necessary to join our essence with the Community of communities, the Divine.

As we become more authentic, more our essential selves, we are able to plant our seeds of community in the fallow, waiting field of potential community. When I look a friend in the eye, pick up my phone and call; when I text, e-mail, write a card, make a date for lunch, I am providing the nourishment of sun and rain, the heat and moisture of growth and connection. These days, for me, all our electronic, instant means of connection, while helpful, never substitute for face-to-face, eye-to-eye contact, and being close enough to touch physically, if we are so moved. A hug can create community.

The lesson here is to trust our instincts. The reasons we take the initiative to reach out and seek community are valid, yet may not result in what we envision; something else may be created. Because we seek in order to find, our community is born out of our intention, our creativity, or longing and passion. We can imagine our possible community, see the potential first, and then create it. We will create our beloved community from two sources. One is the knowledge that connections already exist, and we can embrace them. The second source is the active creative process and work described above to initiate and sustain relationships with like-souled people. And then the creative process is engaged. The outcome may be what we expect, or not; it may be something of equal or greater value than our expectations.

Just as a key to leaving the Victim Triangle is summoning the courage to make the journey away from playing our outdated roles – as the old role of Abbot of the Chaplaincy Institute was for me – so is the creation of your Beloved Community summoning the courage to be your true self. Yes, the world is often lonely, yet as you deepen your trust in your true self, you will attract community members to you.

Remember to allow astonishment and openness to the possibilities of new members showing up from unfamiliar places. They can arrive in new ways, surprise us with their availability, their numbers and their love for us. Some people want to be our friends! This is our community, which we can create as we wish, as it meets our present-day needs and desires. Our community is a living, organic creation, and it changes, flows, moves, shifts, and transforms as we do. Members come and go, yet still some core remains, the core of loving affirmation of who we really are. We are participating members of several, even many, beloved communities. These communities exist at many levels: in time, place, cyberspace, purpose, school, family, work, race, neighborhood, gender, interest, art, sport, touch, travel, history, passion, spirit.

Queen Elisabeth

I remember when the little kids at Collins Brook School, the alternative school I founded, experienced what for many of them was their first loss. The classroom pet, a gerbil named Queen Elisabeth, had died. The small community of eight or so classmates, ages 5–8, created their own funeral ritual. For the hearse, they used a red wagon padded with hay and loaded with their stuffed animals. They dressed up Queen Elisabeth in a red and white ruffled dress and lay her softly on the hay in the wagon. They surrounded her with their favorite stuffed animals, teddy bears, dogs and cats. Then the kids proceeded to pull the funeral wagon out of their classroom, across the lawn and into the middle school English class. They didn't pause, just paraded through and went right back out the door. The little kids were quiet and a bit afraid to enter the teenagers' classroom, but they did so anyway. The older kids stopped what they were doing and watched, surprised, as the wagon was pulled right down the middle of their tables and chairs. Then the funeral procession made its way over to the school kitchen and dining room. Again, they went right through the middle of the room. Eventually, the kids pulled Queen Elisabeth's wagon back outside and across the lawn to a shady spot under a tree. With determination, they dug a hole; some used some shovels, some used their hands. They argued quietly how big the hole should be. When they decided it was the right size, two of them tenderly unloaded Queen Elisabeth from the wagon, and gently laid her in the hole. One child said, "Goodbye, Queen Elisabeth. Thank you." All of them took turns putting the dirt carefully on top of her body. That was it. They were done. They returned to their classroom. The next day, it turned out that one of their classmates had been sick the day before and had missed Queen Elisabeth's funeral. So, because they knew that he too loved Queen Elisabeth, the kids, with his help, got the wagon out again and took it over to Queen Elisabeth's grave. In a very business-like, yet loving manner, they dug her up, brushed her off and put her carefully back in the red wagon. Then they recreated the whole funeral procession, parading a second time through the whole school, then brought her back to the grave under the tree, cleaned out the hole, and buried her all over again. When the community of little kids realized that one of their members had missed an important ritual, they cared enough about their classmate, and Queen Elisabeth, to include him the next day. Both funeral processions, especially the second one, really impressed the teenagers! The image of Queen Elisabeth lingers with me too, the small brown furry body so loved by the little kids, and such a teacher of reverence, and gratitude, and community.

Creation's Community

We are part of an infinite ever-expanding community, the Cosmos, which is all the time growing into more and more complexity. Each community, a circle of members, is a Creation, and its cells continue to grow and seek out other circles with which to connect and relate. Creation itself can be seen as a web of circles of circles, networks of networks, a vast organic evolution. The more communities we discover in which to participate or create ourselves, the more the boundaries melt away to reveal communion and oneness. We are one because we are all part of Creation, the ultimate Beloved Community.

Spiritual Practice: "My Tribe"

Find a quiet space and sit in silence, relax into this present moment. Realize that you have access to all the air and energy you need, that you are held and supported by the earth underneath you. In your mind's eye, call forth individuals that cared for you in the past, people both in and outside your blood family:

your beloved community, your tribe, your family and friends, near and far, alive and deceased. If you can't find any, imagine who you would like to have in your tribe and invite them forward. Bring these individuals, and perhaps animals as well, into your heart and allow yourself to feel the deep affections and affirmations they offer you. Let their love shower over and into you; nourish your being with their love. Feel the warmth of their support and good wishes. Let this sink deeply into your core. Know that their love is with you, now and always. Allow your community to love you.

Chapter 14

Essence: Naked and Empty

Meditation:
The wooden mallet strikes the singing bowl.
The sweet sound calls us into meditation.
Now the sound slowly fades into empty silence, leaving all the space
we need for our own silence.

The phrase 'Naked and Empty' originated for me when a teacher for a Chaplaincy Institute of Maine class called me several hours before class and said she couldn't make it to teach that night and I agreed to take her place. I showed up for the class and acknowledged I was not the assigned teacher and had little background to teach the scheduled topic. When the class began, I said to the students that I felt "Naked and Empty". I went on to describe other situations in which I had found myself, with little notice or preparation, asked to teach or provide spiritual care. Gradually, over time, I developed a certain confidence and freedom in new situations. Yes, I still feel anxious, but I know now it is just energy. Naked and empty, I am not bound by content or topic. I came to trust myself, and what I had to spontaneously offer. My honest admission that I was unprepared set the tone for the class. Together, we dove into the immediacy and democracy of the class, and shared the intimacy of being naked and empty together.

The lesson here is that to live an authentic life – a life of essence – is not a role we play, but a life we lead. As we saw in the chapter on leaving the Victim Triangle, we can't *plan* to be authentic; we either are or we're not. We cannot be ourselves when we are playing roles, using someone else's ideas and words. In the present moment of need, crisis, or spiritual questioning, the most useful tool is our awake and aware presence, our singular ability to trust that God or Spirit is present with us to provide support, assistance and inspiration. Our most awake and aware presence is created when we let go of our agendas, obsessions and projections – become naked and empty – so that we are open to meet the needs of others. The Divine encourages us, literally gives us courage, to be who we are, our authentic selves, and in this purified state, to offer our compassion.

The New Post Office

Another example of being naked and empty happened one day when I had a letter to mail. I walked to our local Post Office branch. This is a small local ice cream shop and video store that had just added postal services. I opened the door and stepped inside to find three men in gray business suits. They stood over by the counter rather formally in a semi-circle, with the new owners, a middle-aged couple from the neighborhood. We were startled to come face to face, though with the letter in my hand it must have been obvious what I was doing there. I felt that I had interrupted something. I looked around and guessed I'd walked in on some sort of opening meeting for the new post office branch. I opened my mouth to speak, and out came the words, "Hi, I'm a minister." They all looked at me, and after a pause one of the men said, "Would you say a prayer?" So I gave a brief spontaneous blessing to handle the postal patrons' precious mail carefully, and to honor the trust placed in postmasters' hands. I imagined out loud the value of a birthday card received or a needed check arriving in time. I said, "Amen." Then I handed my letter to the couple and left. Though time has passed, I still appreciate that event every time I go down to that post office to mail a letter. Even if the postal clerk is a different person, I smile remembering the spontaneous blessing I offered. Like all blessings, it blessed both the receiving people, and the person who spoke the words of blessing.

Earning Integrity

When I begin to teach a class or a training program, I tell the students or volunteers that they must take the ideas and skills I am presenting first for themselves. They must take what is presented, try it on for themselves, and apply it to their own lives first. Then and only then will they truly understand the ideas. If something doesn't fit, or if they don't understand it, they can put it on a 'shelf' and retrieve it later for another look. To consider the idea for themselves, and to apply it to their own life is to earn the integrity to use the ideas and skills with other people. It does not work to sit with a client or patient, a friend or family member when they are in crisis, and need emotional and spiritual support, to say, "Oh, excuse me for a moment." Then we try to remember what a teacher said or we search for a favorite book so we can repeat someone else's words or ideas. No, the offering must come from us, from our own heart and experience. The words must be our own. To the extent that we have something helpful to share beyond our presence, as from a teacher or book, it must flow from our own experience, integrated. When experience is passed through the heart, it becomes wisdom. This process of learning and integration is lifelong. It is how we earn the integrity to work with other people, how we put our experience, care and love into action. Then we offer our true self, and there is no greater gift.

Nick

Another naked and empty encounter happened when I visited my daughter in Connecticut where she is a teacher. We have a family tradition that my wife and I visit our daughter's fourth grade classroom every spring. We spend the whole school day in the classroom, and have the great pleasure of seeing her work with her students. Our daughter gives each of us time to teach something to the students. I usually choose a meditation or art project. After a busy day, we drove back to our daughter's home in a rural area about an hour away. The countryside is dotted with scattered houses and a few remaining farms. When her husband came home from work, we stood in their driveway to discuss where we might go to dinner. A sudden crash interrupted our conversation. The sound came from just up the narrow country road. The four of us began to run until we could see a vehicle off the road. My daughter stopped running, and said she couldn't go on, afraid of what she might find. Her mother stopped with her. I paused and many thoughts and feelings raced through my mind. I realized I had a choice, too. I also was scared at what I might find. I am not trained to offer medical help. I might be able to offer emotional or spiritual assistance. All this took a split second. My son-in-law Andrew and I continued and saw a pickup truck in the bushes. Two neighbors were yelling. We got closer and could see that the truck had crashed into a farm tractor that had then rolled over and pinned its driver underneath it. The truck backed off. Frantically, the four of us tried to lift the tractor. It didn't budge. I felt extreme frustration. The neighbors said they had called 911. Andrew went back home to comfort his wife. I crawled underneath the tractor and saw a young man in the grass and dirt. I could see only part of his head, a shoulder and one arm. I reached out, found his hand and gripped it tightly. His skin felt damp and warm. I started to talk to him, and told him that we had called for help. I said that I would stay with him. It was important to me that he know I was with him, and that I was going to be with him until help came. I don't know where the words came from, but they poured out of my mouth, over and over again. Soon I heard a siren in the distance, and I told him I heard it. I noticed that his skin didn't feel warm any more. I kept saying what I hoped were words of connection and encouragement. Then I felt a definite, strong squeeze from his hand. I kept talking to him while I continued to hold his hand, and used the sound of my words to stay connected. What little I could see of his face seemed to be changing color, from pink to something darker, but with the dirt it was hard to tell. I kept speaking to him. The fire engine eventually arrived and slowly backed up to the tractor. The fire crew fastened a chain to the tractor. Everything seemed to be happening in slow motion, much too slowly. The crew pulled the tractor up and back and hoisted it onto wooden blocks. A stretcher was passed down to us. We gently eased the young man onto the stretcher and carried him to the waiting ambulance. I could hear a helicopter landing in the field next door. The ambulance drove into the field and as soon as they loaded him in, the helicopter took off. I stood in the road, stunned. I'm sure I was in some kind of shock. There was nothing to do but walk slowly back to my daughter's house. When I got there, my family was sitting quietly together. I told them what had happened. We shared our feelings of shock and sadness, and concern for the young man and his family. We put together some food for supper, and waited up for the 11 o'clock news on TV. There was a brief story about the accident that said the young man who had been on the tractor was the 16-year-old only son of the neighboring farm family, and that he had been seriously injured. His name was Nick. Eventually we went to bed, but none of us fell asleep for a long time. The next day before breakfast we watched the morning news and found out that Nick had died. The following weekend my daughter and her husband were able to go to the funeral. At the reception they had the opportunity to tell Nick's parents that I had been with Nick under the tractor.

Several years later, I understand that all of us will likely find ourselves, suddenly and unexpectedly, in a similar moment of choice, a naked and empty situation. Of course I wish that the truck hadn't hit Nick's tractor, and that he hadn't died. But the accident did happen, and Nick did die, and I chose to be there under the tractor with him. The element of choice itself is critical. Choice is highly individual and personal, and cannot be judged from the outside. I chose to continue to run down the road, into the unknown, equipped only as I was, naked and empty. I knew that medical skill would probably be needed, but I had none. What I did have was a willingness to help however I could. I could be present as myself, aware of natural emotions and the Spirit beyond the emotional and physical. My family was right to choose to turn back, because that's what they needed to do. When I saw, with however much frustration and anguish, that the neighbors and I couldn't get the tractor off Nick, I did what I could. I believe it was important that I got under the tractor and held Nick's hand. My sense was that he died while I was with him underneath the tractor. I believe knowing someone was with him gave Nick something valuable, the knowledge that he was not alone. Had it been me alone underneath that tractor, it's what I would have wanted: companionship, and a hand to hold. I hope the knowledge that I was with Nick when he died gave his parents some solace and comfort. I don't know if it did. I do know that I am glad I was with Nick. And I know that I reserve the right to make whatever choices come my way, based on what I think and feel at the moment. I know I can decide based on who I am, naked and empty. I know now that I will be guided by what I feel capable of doing and being in the present circumstance. I have a greater trust in what I can offer, and that what I have to offer will in some way be valuable. What I have to offer is my essence.

Being Abbot

After I studied ministry in California, I was excited to share my experiences with friends and colleagues at home in Maine, all the more so because I missed my fellow students and faculty that I had left behind on the West Coast. These conversations grew and became planning meetings for a new chaplaincy school. We formed a Board of Trustees, designed an interfaith ministry and arts-based curriculum, and looked for faculty. We worked hard to write program requirements, design class schedules, develop reading lists, create a Web site and a descriptive brochure. The trustees thought that we needed another year to be fully prepared to admit our first class of students, but I was eager and did not want to wait. I was aware the new school was far from clothed and full, but I was willing to be naked and empty. I asked the trustees if we could open in a few months. They agreed, and appointed me as the Executive Director. The title didn't sound right to me. The words smacked of hierarchy and false authority. I meditated and prayed about what the leader of this new school might rightfully be named. I discovered in the history of religious schools and monasteries the title Abbot. The more I heard it the more I resonated with it. In addition to signifying the head of a school or monastery, it means father, and I acknowledged I was the father of the school. I asked the Trustees to name my position Abbot and they agreed. I felt that to give the head of our school the title of Abbot gave the school, which after all was a seminary, a distinct identity as a spiritual school.

As the Chaplaincy Institute approached the conclusion of our second year and the pioneer class of students prepared for their Ordination, and the school's inaugural Ordination, I became anxious about the ceremony. This was, after all, our 'coming out' party. We had never done this before. The original ten brave students who had signed up two years ago to enroll in a brand new school now numbered only four. Some had dropped out, some had been asked to leave. One of the senior students had convinced his pastor to host our graduation and ordination ceremony in his country church. I was up most of the night before to deal with a student who, at the last minute, had not completed her graduation requirements, and I had to tell her she could not graduate with her class the next day. I felt sad and frustrated, and even more anxious about the ordination. Because this was the school's first ordination ceremony we had many decisions to make and details to put in place. As the afternoon arrived, the students gathered in the church parish hall adjacent to the sanctuary, the excitement and confusion mounted. We had invited local clergy to attend, and of course our faculty was present. I planned to offer a prayer as we assembled prior to the procession into the church. The time approached, and in the chaos I couldn't find my minister's robe that I had hung up when I first arrived an hour or so ago. People were milling around, getting their robes on, and I couldn't remember where I'd put my own robe. I looked around the room and saw the word Abbot. With relief, I walked over and discovered my robe. I had used a hanger from a local dry cleaning company named Pratt Abbott, and the word Abbot was showing and directed me to my robe. I put it on, and gathered people together. I offered the prayer, then we walked in silence around to the front of the church and climbed the steps into the sanctuary. I was concentrating on the procession; I wanted to get our students and faculty in their right places and up to the front of the church. When I finally reached my chair and turned around, I was astonished. What I saw before me was a full church. A sea of faces looked up at me expectantly. It was at that moment when I realized that this ceremony was not only the ordination of the school's first class of interfaith ministers, but also the ordination of the school itself, and I had stepped fully into the position of the school's Abbot. To find my Abbot's robe in the mystical way that I did confirmed for me my place as the school's spiritual leader.

When I had been running the Chaplaincy Institute of Maine for five or six years, I began to hear a small, still voice inside that was whispering to me, "Be careful! You're becoming somebody." Soon I realized that my essence was being crowded, and perhaps was in danger of being obscured. The accumulating details of administrating the school threatened to overwhelm my spiritual practices. That small, still voice became insistent. I remembered my uncle and mentor, who was headmaster of a New England prep school for years, tell me that he didn't think it was healthy for a school to be run by the same person for a long time, and that he himself didn't want to be closely linked to one school for most of his teaching life. I resonated with those feelings. Second, I was becoming uncomfortable with being Abbot. Part of it was my discomfort living with other people's projections. Often their idea of Abbot was different than mine, and I grew tired of correcting them. A friend suggested that I could move into being Abbot-at-large. I took this potential evolution, and the need to have any title, into prayer and meditation. I looked at my current and evolving spiritual path. The answer became clear. I told the school Trustees that I wanted to step down from being Abbot. I not only felt more and more comfortable with being naked and empty, I saw it as necessary for my spiritual health.

The Stars

When my friend and colleague Andrew Harvey invited a group of spiritual teachers and ministers to join him to co-design a new school to train sacred activists, I accepted and signed up for a yearlong series of weekend planning workshops in Chicago. I attended the first two weekends that fall and winter then realized that even though I had enjoyed the meetings, the spark of excitement was missing. Andrew had definite ideas for the new school's curriculum and the group concentrated on those subjects, at the expense, it seemed to me, of building and sustaining the community. I was disappointed to feel like an outsider. I reluctantly traveled to the last weekend only to fulfill my promise to Andrew. It was telling that on the way to Chicago I missed my flight connection and arrived too late for the first evening presentation. When I did arrive, I discovered that our group had more new members, and I again felt on the outside, not sure what I was doing there. On the second day, Andrew led an exercise in which we would, one at a time, choose a partner, join them to meditate briefly, then share with each other whatever emerged. He asked me to begin. Without thinking, I chose one of the new members, a man named Joe I had only seen across the room on the first day. I sat in front of him, and we looked into each other's eyes. I was supposed to share what came up in my awareness, but no words came. I continued to look into Joe's eyes. We sat in silence. I felt a deep connection, and refrained from breaking it with any words, even though I had been directed to speak with him. Then, his eyes filled with tears. Both of us remained quiet. Tears poured down his face. Soon I was crying too, stunned and opened by the deep and silent connection I felt with Joe. We stayed this way as the group looked on and did not interrupt what was happening. Some minutes later, as Joe and I remained in silence, Andrew, with obvious respect, thanked us. The group moved on to the next partners. That evening Joe and I sat together at dinner. I was interested to learn that he was an astrologer. When I returned home from the workshop, I still felt confused and anxious about leaving my role as Abbot of the Chaplaincy Institute of Maine, even more so because I had new appreciation for the school's strengths. I called Joe and asked him to give me an astrological reading. I was curious what the stars had to say about resigning as Abbot. We arranged an astrological consultation by telephone. The reading was very helpful to me, showed me that my work leading the school was over and I needed to acknowledge that. Meeting Joe guided me through a major life transition. I was able to make clear plans for my eventual retirement from the Institute. To move away from running the school, to not be identified by a title, did make me feel naked and empty. Yet it offered me a kind of simplicity, a purification for which I longed. Now, with hindsight, and help from the stars, I understand my real reason for joining Andrew's community was not to help him start his school but to help me leave the one I had started.

Perfume

Even in the enormous space and freedom of being naked and empty, the past lingers like the faint perfume of flowers from the garden through which we have just walked. It is said that when we offer a rose to someone, a bit of the fragrance, a whiff of essence, stays with us. Certain perfumes are named "Essence of..." So it is with our feelings as we entrust them to the Universe: our individual perfume joins the garden of creation. *My* feelings become *our* feelings. Our natural emotions, at first unwanted, awkward and sometimes terrifying, become enlivened and enlivening as they insist on their individual purposes. Expressed, our emotions open up pathways to our spirit, to heal and transform us, to reveal our essence.

In the end, for this is the end, at least of this moment, and this book, may your essence, as you find it and express it, live with both abundant peace and ceaseless passion. The combination of inner work and outer action, interior essence expressed as exterior essence, is desperately needed in this time of great chaos and transformation. May your essence flower forth from the limitless creativity of the Universe and shower our ailing planet and its suffering people with tender compassion and heartfelt love. May you have the courage to live your essence, naked and empty, so that nothing holds you back from a direct path to the Divine. May you live with the realization that union with the Divine is not only possible, but also impossible to avoid. Blessed be your essence.

Spiritual Practice: "Naked and Empty"

Sit in meditation without wearing any clothes. Allow yourself to be naked and empty. This of course has both real and symbolic meaning and value. You will need to insure that you are warm enough. Turn up the heat or wear a blanket if you need to. Be as physically naked as you can be. With your mind's awareness scan your whole physical being, beginning at your head and moving down slowly to your legs and feet. Notice any areas of discomfort and send reassurance and comfort to them. When judgments come, let them go. Let the light of your attention and awareness send warmth and comfort to your whole body, one part at a time, culminating in the experience that your whole body is cared for and loved in this moment. Now let your attention move slowly and gently to your mind. Allow your thoughts to come and go, to quietly melt away as they come, so that they slip away leaving you naked and empty. Let the words "naked and empty" be your mantra for the rest of this meditation practice.

Acknowledgements

Meditation:
Let my silence be a gift to my friends
And in this dear moment
To you dear Lord,
Oh Holy Silent One.

I am grateful for the love and support of my wife, Kristine, and for the blended family we created together: our children Sarah, Kreschell, Alexis and Nathan. I appreciate the ongoing love of my sisters, Lea, Molly, and my brother, Doug. I honor my parents for their long-standing encouragement. In my journey towards healing, wholeness and a spiritual perspective, I have been particularly blessed and encouraged by some family members who have had the courage to do their own personal healing work, so that as family members with similar histories, we walk similar paths. Having this support within my own family has made a world of difference, particularly as our elders fade from our lives and our children become adults with their own healing work to do. With the arrival of my first granddaughter, Adi, healing work, the world's and mine, feels all the more important. Adi's mother gave me a small Tibetan singing bowl that I use for meditation when I travel. Now I bring it whenever I visit my granddaughter. Adi likes the ringing tone it makes, and associates it with me and with stillness; I hope she will join me in meditating soon.

The ideas and practices in this book originated from many sources, including Fritz and Laura Perls, Elisabeth Kübler-Ross, the Buddhist traditions, Matthew Fox, Clarissa Pinkola-Estés, Paul Hawken, Eckhart Tolle, Andrew Harvey and Ken Wilber, among others. They became the core teachings for my workshops on grief, Volunteer Trainings at Hospices, the Center for Grieving Children, and the first-year curriculum of the Chaplaincy Institute of Maine – The Year of Contemplation, presentations on Interfaith Spiritual Practices and the Emotional Path to Spirit.

I found these teachers – or they found me – because they embodied my own emerging values and provided inspiration, support and direction. These dear people, for I experienced them as practicing what they preached, offered me the understanding of the role of emotions in developing spirit. They gave me the saving and comforting gift of companionship, and, as well, a strong sense of optimism and hope. I am deeply appreciative.

I feel profound gratitude to the following people for their inspiration: Robert Frost, Frederick Buechner, A.S. Neill, the students & faculty of Collins Brook School, George Cloutier, Niela Horn, Ed & Sonia Nevis, Joe Melnick, Mary Oliver, Matthew Fox, Clarissa Pinkola-Estés, Elisabeth Kübler-Ross, Larry & Ann Lincoln, Nancy Mullins, other Elisabeth Kübler-Ross Center staff members and all the courageous workshop participants. For their friendship I thank Gina Rose Halpern, Bill Hemmens, Michael Dwinell, Rick Rudolph, Mike Miles, Andrew Harvey, Russill Paul, Karen Wentworth, Coleman Barks, Dick Tryon, Henry Warren and Barbara Eberhardt.

For taking our friendship to a new level of honesty and love by reading all or parts of this book and offering their heartfelt and valuable comments, I thank Larry Dossey, Gregg Levoy, Ken Hamilton, Megan Don, Patricia Keel, Bob Atkinson, Susanna Macomb, Nancy Reuben, Ben Fowler, Anne Lynch, Robert Zucker, Sue Young, Roz Leiser, Cindy Castleman, Dana Sawyer, Corinne Martin, Ron Feintech, Gus and Joanne Jaccaci, Arthur Fink, Kitsy Winthrop, Phil Goldberg, Reid Stevens, Ashok Nalamalapu, Eva Goetz, and Phyllida Anam-Áire. To be sure, the responsibility is mine for any errors and mistakes in the book.

To those who put their emotional and spiritual work into service, I honor my Hospice colleagues and volunteers, the Center for Grieving Children staff and volunteers, and my colleagues at the Chaplaincy Institute of Maine: Patricia Ellen, Angie Arndt, Cathy Grigsby, Joel Grossman, Anna Smulowitz, Katie Moody, Sarah Shepley, and Guan DoJo. And ChIMe's brave students. I may have inadvertently omitted some people and for this I apologize. To have such skilled and loving companions on this spiritual journey is a blessing for which I give a deep bow of thanks.

Spiritual Practice: "On Your Side"

Sit for a minute in silence and bring to mind the individuals, family members, friends and colleagues who have provided you with encouragement, love and support over the years, people who are on your side. Picture their faces shining with their blessings for you, their eyes beaming soft love to you. Allow yourself to receive the love they offered you – and still offer you – as it pours forth from their being to yours. If no one comes to mind, imagine your ideal support people, individuals who might care for you. Open to soak in what they give to you. Now activate your energy to thank them for their continuing gifts to you. Express your gratitude to them. Do the best you can to let them know how much you appreciate their help and support.

Epilogue

I hope to help people find and bring forth their precious essence, and share it with the world. I have come to appreciate people who can look me in the eye, get beyond daily trivia and life's distractions to speak the truth about themselves, reflect the love of the divine, people who live in the present moment, awake, aware, conscious and engaged. Still, I know that daily trivia and life's distractions are also the meat and tofu of the spiritual world. I need as companions courageous people who will live as spirits, in the spiritual world wherever it is, wherever they find and create it; I know the world needs such courageous people, and I need them. I hope this book can inspire awakened hearts and people living in and from their essence.

Afterword

Included here is a chart of what fuels and frees us from the Victim Triangle from Chapter 8, questions expanded from Chapter 9 on spiritual belief systems, followed by two writings to use to strengthen your spiritual practice. One is an example from the Morning Blessing Letter Project, my thesis to complete my Doctor of Ministry program at the University of Creation Spirituality. The other is a visualization inspired by my love of the Maine coast.

FUELS VICTIM TRIANGLE	WAYS OUT OF VICTIM TRIANGLE
Denial	Response-ability
Any substance abuse	Living clean and sober
Avoidance	Directness
Blaming	Accepting responsibility
"You" statements	"I" statements
Abandoning your inner child	Honoring your inner child
Withholding feelings	Expressing feelings
Confusion	Awareness
Isolation	Community
Co-dependency	Assertiveness
Rigidity	Flexibility
Fakeness	Authenticity
Saying "yes" when you mean "no"	Saying "yes" when you mean "yes"
Saying "no" when you mean "yes"	Saying "no" when you mean "no"
Lose-lose interactions	Win-win interactions
Conditional love	Unconditional love
Lack of discipline	Firm, consistent discipline
Deceit	Honesty
Hide spirituality	Show spirituality

Questions on Your Spiritual Nature

What words and images remind you that you are a spiritual being?

Where in your home does your spirit show?

When are you most likely to feel your spirit?

Which people in your life evoke or encourage your spirituality?

Are there foods and/or drinks that have a spiritual meaning for you?

Who are your spiritual guides? What are their names? How do you communicate with them?

What religion or wisdom tradition supports your spiritual life?

When your head hits the pillow at the end of the day, what gives your day meaning?

What in nature calls forth your spirit? Any particular place?

What time of day or night do you pray, meditate, ask to be guided, etc?

How do you meditate?

What is your goal of meditation?

What do you believe in?

How do you pray? And to whom or what? Do you seek results?

What colors are spiritual for you?

With which of your friends do you share your spirituality? How?

How do you express your spirit and spirituality?

What do you hope and dream for?

What are you most afraid of?

Who or what were you before you were 'born' and will you be after you 'die'?

What sounds and music are spiritual for you?

What forms of art inspire your spirit?

Which of your ancestors' spirits are you attuned to?

What daily activities express your spiritual nature?

How do you share your spirit with family or friends, or colleagues at work?

What animals does your spirit relate to?

Who do you love, and who loves you?

Is your spirit likely to express more in solitude or in groups of people?

Which emotions encourage your spirit to emerge?

What roles must you shed to uncover your spirit?

What is the 'still small voice' inside you saying?

What are your current spiritual practices?

Select the questions that resonate for you, and let the others go. I suggest you choose one question to take into meditation. You can write your responses in your journal.

Morning Blessing Letters

I originally began writing Morning Blessing Letters as my own meditation first thing every morning. For a period of six months, I wrote one every weekday morning, in the meditative quiet of the new day, before breakfast. As soon as a Morning Blessing Letter was finished, I e-mailed it to a list of colleagues and friends. Every letter was written in a carefully designed form to wake up, encourage and support health care workers and chaplains in their daily work with patients and caregivers. I also hand distributed them every week to hospitals and agencies, and to counselors and therapists in Portland.

Each Morning Blessing Letter has seven focusing paragraphs:

1. Welcome
2. Silent meditation
3. Affirmation of physical self
4. Affirmation of emotional self
5. Affirmation of spiritual self
6. A specific blessing or intention for the day
7. A gift for the day

I encourage you to use each paragraph to center yourself in the morning, giving loving attention to each part of yourself as an intentional and practical way to nurture your whole being at the beginning of the day. I offer this particular Morning Blessing Letter, which I wrote a decade ago, as a specific tool to deepen and support your spiritual practice to live your essence:

Morning Blessing Letter

Welcome as this day dawns. Open to it through a child's eyes. Let go of "knowing" what this day will bring. Who really knows? Stay with the slight anxiety of not knowing, which is really only energy, energy for this day of yours.

Be here in your new day in silence, the silence of creation. Let go of anticipation, the things of life, and be here in this silence, life itself...

Recognize that for now you live your life in this body, your temple this time. Notice it, feel it, inhabit it. Awaken it by feeling it now: your feet that ground you on this earth, your legs, your thighs, your belly, your chest, your arms to handle your world, your head and face, that give and receive so much.

Your emotions surface from the deep well, bubbling up to be expressed into the universe. There is no stopping them. Like lava they burn their own path, one way or another. Do not resist them, but welcome your feelings.

As your feelings well up, so comes a second, deeper force. Your soul, that which is most you, you in purest from, now has the way clear. As basic as your breath, your soul is your life itself. Be your soul.

Enter this day open from the inside out. May you find the courage to be outside who you are inside, all one. May you bring your essence to the world today.

Your gift today is essence.

Fog

A visualization

Here in Maine, the thick wet fog rolls slowly in from the Atlantic Ocean. The fog gathers density from the white surf breaking on the hard black rocks, first at the outermost islands: towering Monhegan, then low and long Damariscove Island, safe haven for the men and women of the coast's first fishing community. Then the fog moves on south down to the hulk of Sequin Island, then to tiny Halfway Rock with its tall stone lighthouse. After touching stately Jewell Island and the rest of the Calendar Islands, the fog lumbers onto the mainland at Portland, touching and enveloping all of us. Just as the fog is all around us, we are surrounded and touched and loved by the spirits of all who have ever walked this earth. Allow yourself now, as you hear these words in the present moment, to know and to feel this spiritual blanket surrounding you like fog. Now, as you breathe, you take in the thick texture of love and goodwill. So it is at this very moment, here and now. See how you welcome that which is already here, already yours. Use your five senses: sight, touch, hearing, smell, taste and the sixth, intuition. Now, here you arrive, where you can live your life today. Now, finally you have arrived in your life and can be a part of it all. Now you can know and feel and enjoy and celebrate your being, leaving behind loneliness, embracing the fog as it embraces you. Be yourself without being alone, but with your self being surrounded by all the love you will ever need, ever.

Resources

After teaching a class or completing a training workshop, I am often asked for reading suggestions. I am reluctant to suggest any. It is more likely to be helpful if the student finds his or her own source of information and inspiration, and more importantly, if the student activates his or her own interior resources. However, here are a few resources I have found helpful.

Books

Dass, Ram. *Paths to God: Living the Bhagavad Gita*. Harmony Books. New York. 2004

Fox, Matthew. *Original Blessing: A Primer in Creation Spirituality*. Bear & Co. Santa Fe, NM. 2003

Greenspan, Miriam. *Healing Through the Dark Emotions: The Wisdom of Grief, Fear, and Despair*. Shambhala. Boston. 2003

Harvey, Andrew. *The Direct Path: Creating a Journey to the Divine Using the World's Mystical Traditions*. Broadway Books. New York. 2000

Hawken, Paul. *Blessed Unrest: How the Largest Movement in the World Came into Being and Why No One Saw It Coming*. Penguin. New York. 2007

Levoy, Gregg. *Callings: Finding and Following an Authentic Life*. Three Rivers Press. New York. 2009

Myss, Caroline. *Anatomy of the Spirit: The Seven Stages of Power and Healing*. Crown Publishers. New York. 1996

Teasdale, Wayne. *Mystic Heart: Discovering a Universal Spirituality in the World's Religions*. New World Library. Novato, CA. 2001

Tolle, Eckhart. *A New Earth: Awakening to Your Life's Purpose*. Dutton. New York. 2005

Wilber, Ken. *The Simple Feeling of Being: Embracing Your True Nature*. Shambhala. Boston. 2004

Songs

"As Long As You Love", "A Thousand Shades of Grey" – Cindy
Bullens, *Somewhere Between Heaven and Earth*
"Celebration of the Moment" – Deuter, *Sea and Silence*
"Cup of Kindness" – Emmylou Harris, *Stumble Into Grace*
"How Could Anyone" – Shaina Noll, *Songs for the Inner Child*
"If I Could Be Where You Are" – Enya, *Songs For Japan*, Disc 2
"Thank You For Hearing Me", "What Doesn't Belong To Me" –
Sinead O'Connor, *Faith and Courage*
"The Living Years" – Mike and the Mechanics, *Living Years*
"Turning Toward the Morning" – Gordon Bok, *Before Their Time*,
Volume 1
"You're Missing" – Bruce Springsteen, *The Rising*
"Will You Remember Me" – Rosanne Cash, *Rules of Travel*

Organizations

A World Alliance of Interfaith Clergy: awainterfaithclergy.org
Center for Grieving Children: cgcmaine.org
Chaplaincy Institute: chaplaincyinstitute.org
Chaplaincy Institute of Maine: chimeofmaine.org
Creation Spirituality Communities: originalblessing.ning.com
Externalization workshops: externalizationworkshops.com,
Growthandtransition.com, transitionsworkshops.com
Institute for Sacred Activism: andrewharvey.net
Soundstrue.com
Wisdom University: wisdomuniversity.org

About the Author

Rev. Jacob Watson, D.Min. is an interfaith minister and spiritual teacher. He helped start Collins Brook School, and the Center for Grieving Children, where he designed and delivered the Volunteer Training Program, and continues to train volunteers. Since 1985 he has been a Hospice Volunteer, Chaplain, Board member, trainer and chaplain supervisor. He was a grief counselor in private practice, and a senior staff member of the Elisabeth Kübler-Ross Center, leading Life, Death and Transition workshops nationally and overseas. He teaches classes on Spirituality and Healing, and The Emotional Path to Spirit at the University of Southern Maine and other venues. Jacob is a graduate of the University of Creation Spirituality and the Chaplaincy Institute for Arts and Interfaith Ministries, and is the founding Abbot of the Chaplaincy Institute of Maine. He is the author of *Morning Blessing Letters: A Book of Daily Gifts*, articles on grief and spiritual care, and offers workshops and individual spiritual companionship.

Rev. Jacob Watson, D.Min.
41 Glenwood Avenue
Portland, Maine 04103
207-761-2522
jacobw@gwi.net
www.revjacobwatson.com

Also by Jacob Watson
Morning Blessing Letters: A Book of Daily Gifts

BOOKS

O is a symbol of the world, of oneness and unity; this eye
represents knowledge and insight. We publish titles on
general spirituality and living a spiritual life. We aim to
inform and help you on your own journey in this life.

Visit our website: http://www.o-books.com

Find us on Facebook:
https://www.facebook.com/OBooks

Follow us on Twitter: @obooks